# Designing and Evaluating Usable Technology in Industrial Research

Three Case Studies

# Synthesis Lectures on Human-Centered Informatics

### Editor
**John M. Carroll**, *Penn State University*

Human-Centered Informatics (HCI) is the intersection of the cultural, the social, the cognitive, and the aesthetic with computing and information technology. It encompasses a huge range of issues, theories, technologies, designs, tools, environments and human experiences in knowledge work, recreation and leisure activity, teaching and learning, and the potpourri of everyday life. The series will publish state-of-the-art syntheses, case studies, and tutorials in key areas. It will share the focus of leading international conferences in HCI.

**Designing and Evaluating Usable Technology in Industrial Research: Three Case Studies**
**Clare-Marie Karat and John Karat**
**2010**

**Interacting with Information**
**Ann Blandford, Simon Attfield**
**2010**

**Designing for User Engagement: Aesthetic and Attractive User Interfaces**
**Alistair Sutcliffe**
**2009**

**Context-Aware Mobile Computing: Affordances of Space, Social Awareness, and Social Influence**
**Geri Gay**
**2009**

**Studies of Work and the Workplace in HCI: Concepts and Techniques**
**Graham Button, Wes Sharrock**
**2009**

**Semiotic Engineering Methods for Scientific Research in HCI**
**Clarisse Sieckenius de Souza, Carla Faria Leitão**
**2009**

**Common Ground in Electronically Mediated Conversation**
**Andrew Monk**
**2008**

Designing and Evaluating Usable Technology in Industrial Research: Three Case Studies
Clare-Marie Karat and John Karat


ISBN: 978-3-031-01062-0      paperback
ISBN: 978-3-031-02190-9      ebook


DOI 10.1007/978-3-031-02190-9


A Publication in the Springer series
*SYNTHESIS LECTURES ON HUMAN-CENTERED INFORMATICS*

Lecture #7
Series Editor: John M. Carroll, *Penn State University*
Series ISSN
Synthesis Lectures on Human-Centered Informatics
Print 1946-7680    Electronic 1946-7699

# Designing and Evaluating Usable Technology in Industrial Research

**Three Case Studies**

Clare-Marie Karat and John Karat
IBM T.J. Watson Research Center

*SYNTHESIS LECTURES ON HUMAN-CENTERED INFORMATICS #7*

# ABSTRACT

This book is about HCI research in an industrial research setting. It is based on the experiences of two researchers at the IBM T. J. Watson Research Center. Over the last two decades, Drs. John and Clare-Marie Karat have conducted HCI research to create innovative usable technology for users across a variety of domains. We begin the book by introducing the reader to the context of industrial research as well as a set of common themes or guidelines to consider in conducting HCI research in practice. Then case study examples of HCI approaches to the design and evaluation of usable solutions for people are presented and discussed in three domain areas:

- Conversational speech technologies,

- Personalization in eCommerce, and

- Security and privacy policy management technologies

In each of the case studies, the authors illustrate and discuss examples of HCI approaches to design and evaluation that worked well and those that did not. They discuss what was learned over time about different HCI methods in practice, and changes that were made to the HCI tools used over time. The Karats discuss trade-offs and issues related to time, resources, and money and the value derived from different HCI methods in practice. These decisions are ones that need to be made regularly in the industrial sector. Similarities and differences with the types of decisions made in this regard in academia will be discussed.

The authors then use the context of the three case studies in the three research domains to draw insights and conclusions about the themes that were introduced in the beginning of the book. The Karats conclude with their perspective about the future of HCI industrial research.

# KEYWORDS

HCI, industrial research, case studies, conversational speech technologies, personalization, security, privacy, policy management technologies

*This book is dedicated to Zachary Alexander Karat,*
*whose curiosity about the world, and zest for life,*
*keep his mom and dad young at heart.*

# Contents

# Acknowledgments

We wish to express our appreciation for the HCI book series editor, Jack Carroll, and the Morgan and Claypool editor Diane Cerra for their contributions to the completion of this book.

Clare-Marie Karat and John Karat
January 2010

# Preface

Research in industrial laboratories in the information technology sector provides human-computer interaction (HCI) professionals an environment to work on real-world and futuristic challenges and opportunities. HCI researchers can address current, pressing issues as well as consider visions of the future. In industry, there is an expectation that at some point, the valuable discoveries and new technologies that result from such research can be brought to the marketplace as new or enhanced products and services to improve people's lives.

This book provides a glimpse into the HCI profession in an industrial laboratory setting through an examination of three case studies. The authors have each worked at the IBM T. J. Watson Research Center for over twenty years, and the case studies reported here represent a sampling of three lines of HCI research conducted during that time that we consider both significant and illustrative. We hope that the reader finds the case studies enlightening, both in illustrating the value of various HCI approaches we have employed at different times, and in understanding the context of industrial research itself which sets the parameters for delivering value to the organization and to society at large.

Clare-Marie Karat and John Karat
January 2010

CHAPTER 1

# Introduction: Themes and Structure of the Book

## 1.1   THE STRUCTURE OF THE BOOK

This book is about HCI research in an industrial research setting. It is based on the experiences of two researchers at the IBM T.J. Watson Research Center. Over the last two decades, Drs. John and Clare-Marie Karat have conducted HCI research to create innovative usable technology for users across a variety of domains.

In this first chapter, we provide a description of the context in which HCI research is conducted in industrial laboratory settings. We then discuss a set of common themes or guidelines for the HCI professional to consider in conducting HCI research in practice. Next, we introduce a set of questions that provide a common format and serve as a guide for the discussion of the case study research in the following chapters. With this common perspective in the description of the case studies, it is possible to compare and contrast the case studies and gain further insight from them.

The three case studies are presented in separate chapters. These case studies cover research in three different domains: conversational speech technologies, personalization in eCommerce, and security and privacy policy management technologies.

Following the case studies, we revisit the opening themes presented here in the introduction and discuss conclusions that can be drawn based on the perspective and insights gained from the content and context of the case studies. We conclude with a few thoughts about the future of HCI research in industry.

## 1.2   THE CONTEXT FOR CONDUCTING HCI RESEARCH IN INDUSTRY

The context in which HCI research, or any other area of IT related research, is conducted in industry may vary from organization to organization; however, there are a set of characteristics which remain fairly common across the labs. First and foremost, the research organization is part of a business, and as such, an industrial research laboratory ultimately has a responsibility to provide business value to the organization it is a part of. It may do so through a variety of means. A research lab can contribute to the invention of new technologies that may be brought to market through new products or services. The research results delivered by the lab might provide incremental advances or create whole new areas of opportunity for the company. The lab can contribute to the intellectual capital of the company through the creation of patents which might detail new technologies or approaches. Such patents can provide a source of revenue or can be used by the company in negotiations with other companies. The research lab can also provide value by providing leadership in professional organizations, which provide direction in research policy and technology standards. Finally, members of a research organization can provide service to the research community through participation in conference and journal activities to advance knowledge in the field, gain knowledge themselves, and educate current and future researchers.

An industrial research laboratory is not a university or a foundation, although it has some aspects of both. Universities have goals that include educating students and conducting research to advance knowledge for its own sake. Foundations provide gifts and grants to promote the good of society. Research laboratories in industry do promote the ongoing education of the scientists and other research team members who work there, including undergraduate and graduate students who join a research team for internships, hosting professors on sabbatical, establishing ongoing project relationships between academic and industry laboratories, and other types of short or longer term collaborations. It is vital to business organizations that their researchers establish and maintain expertise at the leading edge of knowledge in the technical domains of research so the company's research can be shaped by their expertise and the best information available. Having a research lab staffed with people whose expertise is known in the outside community can also be important for attracting future talent to the company. This expertise develops within and across research and development teams within the organization as well as through ongoing interaction with colleagues at universities and in scientific organizations in government.

There is one aspect of collaboration within an industrial research lab that we think sets it apart from our experience of academic research departments. While all organizations have structures which tend to favor collaboration within some units at the cost of collaboration across others, we find the borders are far more easily traversed in industry than in academic contexts. In many cases, we have formed collaborations with researchers in very different areas (e.g., cryptography, security policy analysis) to create solutions. Certainly, this happens in academic contexts as well, but we feel that it is far more common in industrial settings. We would attribute this to a more fluid organizational structure in industry, with "departments" that generally have far less longevity. Perhaps, this is unusual to IBM research, which is a very large organization compared to typical computer science departments in academic settings, and perhaps, it is also facilitated by the nature of HCI research which tends to be very broad and diverse. Regardless, it has had a significant impact on many aspects of our own research in which we have often sought to leverage the research of colleagues involved in more narrowly defined technical topics.

Establishing and maintaining long-term relationships with universities is a win-win situation for both parties as the university students and professors gain experience and knowledge by working with industrial researchers on real customer issues and opportunities, and the academics can contribute and shape the research underway to address these technical areas. The industrial researchers gain from interaction with the students and professors in learning about their interests and research approaches in the university settings. It's a good opportunity for 'cross-pollination' for the people involved in industry and academia.

In industrial research, there are research division and corporate goals that guide the definition of the portfolio of research topics that the scientists pursue. Within the portfolio, there may be a defined goal which calls for a mixture of different types of research. The portfolio will likely contain research with different levels of risk or probability of success, that is, a mixture of research with near-term applicability (research that is fairly low-risk and applied in nature, results may be used in products and services in 1-3 years), mid-term applicability (more open-ended research goals with more risk, somewhat exploratory research, where results may be employed within 5-7 years), and long-term applicability (exploratory, risky, and blue-sky research, where results may be leveraged in the next 10-20 years).

Funding models for research vary. Research funding may originate from both internal and external sources. In some companies, a corporate 'tax' is assigned to the product and services groups, and this funding pool underwrites the research program. In other organizations, product groups fund specific research proposals for a specific period of time with defined goals and expected deliverables. Research teams may also submit proposals in response to government calls for proposals. These external proposals may be created with other academic or industry colleagues. There are also a variety of hybrid approaches using elements of the various models. There will generally be a set of management and review mechanisms in place for research projects to determine their progress towards goals, viability, and the feasibility of continued support for them. Some projects are initiated with multiyear research agendas and funding; for others, there is a requirement to demonstrate quarterly milestones towards year-end deliverables and goals. The parameters of the research are highly context dependent based on the research topic, sponsor, and nature of the goals and deliverables of the particular research project.

There is also a wide range of processes in place in industrial research organizations in terms of leveraging the results of research. In some projects, where the sponsor is funding research to address a particular issue or opportunity, the results may be carefully integrated into a new or updated product or service, with a smooth transition from research to development or services staff. Often, the project team is a mixture of people in these different roles, and the proportion of each group changes on the team as the deliverables move from research to development.

Research results are incorporated in strategy and product planning processes. The results provide valuable data for the organization in deciding whether or not to go forward with a particular product or service at the current time or at a future date when other anticipated changes are likely to provide a higher probability of success. Research results can guide the organization in identifying the niche area or 'sweet spot' for a product or service. The intellectual property patented through research efforts is valuable in the organizations strategy and product planning processes in providing the organization the ability to negotiate with potential business partners on the use of ideas for products and services.

In some industrial research organizations, the research results are 'thrown over the wall' to development, and there are few processes or mechanisms to ensure that the research results are leveraged by the development and services groups. As you may imagine, the ability of the organization to leverage results in this type of environment is highly variable.

Where research is completed for an external sponsor, there are generally contractual obligations that are met through the delivery of interim and final code, design and user documentation, and project reports. Often in these situations, there will be ongoing collaborations between the research groups and the external sponsors, with interaction and communication throughout the project and a transition period when the research staff work closely with the sponsor's team at the end of the project.

Whether an HCI researcher is completing research for an internal or external sponsor, it is critical to understand the goals and the parameters of the project. Available time, resource, and funding provide a framework within which tradeoffs in options towards achieving defined goals can be discussed, and decisions can be made with buy-in from the sponsor. Research in industry is expected to proceed at a rapid pace, and part of the skill required of the HCI expert is to understand what trade-offs are feasible in the pursuit of project goals through use of different approaches in a defined problem space and how different HCI tools and methods might be tailored for use in different contexts.

Good communication with the project sponsor or customer throughout the project and management of the customer's expectations are paramount to success of the HCI research in a project. The design solution that the HCI researcher provides must address the sponsor's concerns and needs, and do so within agreed-upon parameters, or the deliverables may be viewed as of little value. There may be scientific and intellectual property value in the deliverables, and these are beneficial to the organization as a whole, but to be a successful project, the deliverables must meet the needs of the sponsor.

To succeed, the HCI expert must also communicate well and manage the expectations of the management hierarchy within the Research group. The HCI researcher must be able to clearly communicate the value of the particular research project in terms of the scientific advancement, intellectual property, international visibility and leadership in professional organizations, and impact on the business through product and services, as well as through delivery of key research results to external sponsors.

The HCI researcher works within a multifaceted problem space and uses his or her own skill, experience, and creativity as well as that of the multidisciplinary project team to determine the approach to a particular research question. In this context, access to real-world customers is a key factor in success. Interaction with customers provides a wealth of information and ideas about the problem space. The customer perspective about the challenges and opportunities can be insightful. The relationship can provide a very rewarding experience for all involved in terms of learning from each other and seeing new possibilities.

# 1.3   INDUSTRIAL HCI RESEARCH THEMES

Much of what we said in the previous section applies generally to different research fields in industrial research. We will now turn to identifying issues more specific to our own field of inquiry – HCI. There are a set of themes about HCI research in industry that we think will be valuable to consider as you read the book and conduct your own research. This set of three themes is based on our experience and the input from fellow HCI researchers in industry. The themes cover the framing of the HCI research question, the approach to the HCI research, and the different ways in which industrial HCI research can provide value to the organization and society at large.

## 1.3.1   WHAT ARE YOU TRYING TO DO?
### FRAMING THE HCI RESEARCH QUESTION

The first theme is related to one of the most critical steps in HCI research in industry, and that is to appropriately frame the research problem space. The most critical point is to identify and understand the user or target audience requirements related to the activity to be addressed, the relevant characteristics of the people who will perform it, and the social and physical context of use. There are a number of different methods that together help with this key task. One of the best ways to identify user requirements is to work with visionary target customers to understand the problem space. We have found that it is important to consider the source of the funding as an important factor in defining the research plan. Generally, speaking, the sponsor of the research in industry will provide a high-level statement of the research goals, which is more narrowly focused than the calls for proposals issued by academic funding sources (e.g., the National Science Foundation in the United States). Often, the sponsor of the research (either internal – for example, a product division, or external – for example, a government agency) will provide recommendations about potential customers to work with. Once you speak with one customer group, they may recommend peers in other organizations for you to speak with as well, and you can build up a sample of customer contacts.

Getting to know the user is such an obvious first step in the process, but it is one that we find is often given relatively little attention (at best) or simply ignored as unnecessary (at worst). These user/customer interactions may occur over a series of sessions where mutual trust and respect is formed, and a win/win work environment is established where the customer representatives can provide input (e.g., by allowing observation of work processes, through interviews, etc.) and they can see the benefit of their input in the framing of the research question. Researchers can conduct ongoing literature reviews to understand best practices and previous research in the domain under study. The literature reviews can provide the researcher background which enriches the sessions with the customer. Each session with the customer will provide additional insight which informs and enriches the next session as well. Over time and with input from the customer and the sponsor, consensus should be developed about the definition of the research problem space, and the goals, motivation, risks and dependencies in that design space.

It is also critical to realize that in the real world, events happen that change the definition of the HCI problem space during the course of the research. The researcher must be prepared to change requirements, make adjustments, and continue the research within a different set of constraints as warranted. Research in industry contexts is rarely funded with the multi-year commitments more common in academic contexts. While we don't view this as necessarily good or bad, we do think it is important to be aware of it and to plan for how to scope the size of a project and appropriately communicate progress.

### 1.3.2    HOW ARE YOU GOING TO GO ABOUT DOING IT? APPROACHES TO HCI RESEARCH

A second theme in industrial HCI research is concerned with the different alternatives possible in how to approach the HCI research, and the tailoring required for the use of a particular HCI tools in a particular HCI research domain and set of circumstances. For example, after learning how to use a usability walkthrough successfully in HCI research, you can determine how to adapt the walkthrough procedure to different social and physical contexts in a particular setting for the research. You will learn the value of feedback on different types of prototypes and how to maximize the effectiveness of different types of evaluations.

The industrial HCI researcher must be able to make trade-offs and decisions concerning the best methodological approach to the research problem in a particular domain. In part, these types of decisions about the tools and methods to use in a particular study is what all HCI researchers do. The difference in the industrial setting of HCI research is that there is the constant requirement to balance the time, money and resources to address critical research questions in the midst of ongoing changes in the environment. And as mentioned above, a wide variety of events may occur that necessitate adjustments to the plan given unforeseen changes in needs of the business, and the time, money, and resources originally allocated for the research. Our approaches to how we conduct research have evolved over the years – moving from formal methods oriented toward the establishment of certainty of results toward approaches geared toward efficient delivery of context specific insight. Along the way, we have found it valuable to keep track of ways in which we feel there might be limitations in our findings, in case business-driven changes in problem definition arise and we need to rethink our research approach.

### 1.3.3    HOW WILL YOU KNOW YOU HAVE SUCCEEDED? DEMONSTRATING THE VALUE OF THE HCI RESEARCH

The third and last theme that will be a constant drumbeat for the industrial HCI researcher is to be able to demonstrate the positive impact of the industrial HCI research completed. Certainly, any researcher in an industrial research lab must regularly illustrate the value of the research completed, whether that research is on parallel processing performance, chemical polymers, or cloud computing. The point here is that demonstrating value is not generally limited to "when the research is done." Once a project is initiated, there will be frequent requests for reports on how things are going. Establishing a plan of how you might report incremental progress might seem like a nuisance in industrial settings, but providing interim reports can help establish trust with sponsors who might value the manageability of a project more than traditionally considered in academic contexts.

In industry, projects are generally viewed as consisting of a series of deliverables, with schedules developed and managed. We do not propose that such an approach be strictly applied to HCI research, but it is reasonable to make sponsors aware of a range of things that might be provided along the course of an HCI research project. In general, in an industrial research laboratory, the measures of research value for an HCI researcher include:

- External publications of high quality research,

- Transferring research ideas and technology into product and services the organization can provide to customers,

- Filing patents to protect the intellectual property associated with the ideas created through the research,

- Informing the organization's strategy so that business opportunities are leveraged,

- Grass-roots education of managers and co-workers about the value of HCI, and influencing their decisions and actions that lead to positive business outcomes,

- Leadership roles in internal and external professional communities including international conferences, journals, government societies, and standards groups,

- Collaborative research relationships with colleagues in academia, and

- Service to the community through ongoing mentoring of students, science education outreach to schools, volunteer positions in the community, and provision of needed skills and technology during emergency situations.

All of these can provide evidence of the value of the research at different stages in a project, and depending on the specifics of the research, it can be utilized to help communicate where the research is at a point in time and where it is going.

The three themes above will be illustrated as we present the case studies in this book. In order to be successful, the HCI researcher in industry must be able to frame an HCI research problem correctly, select and apply the appropriate HCI method among many to conduct the research and adjust plans in the face of changing circumstances, and then be able to demonstrate the value of that HCI research through a variety of avenues. This is not a career for the faint of heart. HCI researchers are constantly faced with challenges to their "technical" contributions in a field that many mistake as being about technology alone rather than technology in use. It is a challenging career, and also rewarding in terms of being able to make a real impact in solving significant problems and making the world a better place.

## 1.4    COMMON FORMAT FOR THE CASE STUDIES

Before beginning the discussion of the case studies, we would like to orient you to the format for the chapters. The next three chapters will discuss the three case studies in the book. Each chapter will cover a common set of topics that build largely on the themes introduced in the previous section, with the addition of a "Lessons Learned" topic as a fourth discussion area for the case studies. The following key topics to provide a fairly chronological-based discussion of research:

1. Background on the Domain of Study

2. Purpose of the HCI Research

3. Research Approach and Tradeoffs Made

4. HCI Research Results and Impact

5. Lessons Learned from the HCI Research

   After the examination of the three case studies, we will look across the case studies to identify further insights and conclusions.

CHAPTER 2

# Case Study 1: Conversational Speech Technologies: Automatic Speech Recognition (ASR)

## 2.1 BACKGROUND ON THE DOMAIN OF STUDY

We remember seeing a demonstration of a speech recognition prototype in our labs over 25 years ago where someone sat down and spoke "Please write to Mrs. Wright right now." Not only was it wonderful to see words appearing on the screen in response to voice input, but the fact that the system presented three different spellings of the word "Right" seemed magical. A few years later, while working on a study of commercial speech recognition studies, we both had mixed feelings about how far the technology had advanced. From the Control Room, we could feel the frustration of users trying out the technology for the first time. One woman let out a scream as the system responded with the text "topless insane" as she tried to issue the command "Stop Listening." To this day, we do not send out memos dictated to an ASR system without careful proofreading.

As behavioral scientists, we work in the computer field to try to discover ways in which we can make technology better serve human needs. In some naive past, some of us assumed that the introduction of speech recognition and output to interactive systems would undoubtedly improve their usability. We now know that designing computer systems which accept speech as input or use speech as output requires considerable effort. There are several reasons - but the main one is that the technology for recognizing words in speech makes guesses about what you said and sometimes these guesses are wrong. This is fundamentally different than interaction with a keyboard. Systems don't guess what key you pressed. If you type as we do, you might occasionally press a "wrong" key and an "error" might result, but the errors are ones that you make, not ones that the computer makes. We have reduced the frequency of errors in speech recognition software so that many people find speech applications acceptable, but we are a long way from finding our landscapes littered with abandoned, useless keyboards and mice.

Automatic speech recognition (ASR) technology has been under development for over 35 years, with considerable industry and government resources being devoted to developing systems which can translate speech input into character strings or commands. After all of this effort, we are just beginning to see fairly wide application of the technology. It might be possible to interpret this relatively slow penetration of ASR into interfaces for computer systems as an indication that speech is not a good modality for such interfaces, and that efforts to develop ASR are naive in some way. After all, look at how quickly the Internet has spread. While this "good ideas catch on quickly" notion has a lot of appeal, it would be incorrect to use it at this time in considering ASR. Simply put, ASR will be widely used in interacting with computers in the not to distant future. It will not necessarily replace other input modalities, but it will be a very powerful means of human-computer communication.

In the face of many amusing and no so amusing failures, why do we say this? The main reason is that as technology shrinks in size, the value of speech for input and sound for output will make the technology much more important. We can shrink a lot of components so that we are wearing powerful computers on our wrists, but we can not shrink our fingers to type on wristwatch size devices, and there is only so much we can expect of dial size displays.

## 2.2   PURPOSE OF THE HCI RESEARCH

As HCI researchers, how can we facilitate a technology going from promising candidate to successful tool? We think that there are some fundamental factors to keep in mind when considering the value of ASR and how rapidly and widely it will spread. First is the **ongoing development of speech recognition and generation technology** itself. How we go from an acoustic signal to some computationally useful translation of the signal remains technically challenging. Additionally, speech recognition is of course only part of the picture - a complete speech user interface (SUI) might be expected to produce speech as well. We are in a time of significant changes and improvements in our ability to recognize freeform speech and to generate natural sounding speech output. The goals are speaker-independent, continuous-speech recognition and human sounding speech output. These are not so far off as they once were, but we are not there yet. Actually, the technology is being much more successfully used in environments in which the dialog is constrained, where the system is expecting a limited range of responses, than it is for unconstrained tasks like dictation. Recognition rates are excellent if the vocabulary consists of a few commands or of items like numbers.

Second, while we like to think that speech is a natural form of communication, it is misleading to think that this means that it is easy to build interfaces that will provide a natural interaction with a non-human machine. **Speech is not natural for communicating with machines**. The way people use speech in communicating is strongly influenced by our experience in using it with other people. How we might use speech in communicating with machines needs to be considered carefully. Although having no difference between human-human and human-computer communication might be a good goal, it is not one likely to be attainable in the near future. The naturalness of speech communication should be seen as reflecting our experiences in using the modality to communicate with other humans. These people share a great deal of knowledge with the speaker, and that is something that cannot be said of current computers, though there are ongoing efforts to provide machines with broad contextual and social knowledge. A great deal of the naturalness that we take for granted in verbal communication goes away when the listener doesn't understand the meaning of what we say.

Finally, we argue that **it takes time and practice to develop a new form of interaction**. There are some benefits of "traditional" human-computer interaction through a keyboard, mouse, and screen that we should not forget. Human beings are capable of interacting with the world through multiple modalities at the same time. Some times, our hands are more appropriate devices for controlling our environment than our voices. Interestingly, we are discovering that speech for initial text entry, and keyboard and mouse for correction are much more efficient means of text entry than either modality alone. There are also speech recognition systems or telephony applications that have replaced keypad response systems for interactions over the telephone. Many organizations use telephony applications today with constrained speech vocabularies to answer customer or citizen requests or to direct people to the appropriate service representatives.

While it is true that talking on the phone is fairly natural, people still need to learn about interfaces for talking to the phone. Is the phone listening while it is talking or only when it pauses? If I cough, will it think I was trying to say something? But beyond simple efficiency, sometimes we would all prefer silent interaction. Imagine a world in which everyone's watch was announcing "You have mail. Would you like me to read it to you?" We are suggesting that the technology is not valuable, just that it needs careful crafting to become usable and effective in the context of people's lives.

Clearly, there have been considerable improvements in the technology for both speech-to-text recognition and for text-to-speech output. Continuous speech has replaced the isolated word speech that was required for recognition just a few years ago. Systems are able to differentiate between text and commands in dictation, speaker independence in use of tools is moving closer to reality, and there is incremental progress in producing more natural sounding output. Problems remain with the current generation of large vocabulary desktop dictation products. However, it is not very "far out" to imagine dictating an e-mail note in English and having the system translate it and read it back to the user in French. We can now move beyond having to exaggerate the usefulness of speech in the interface to focusing on how this improved technology can become as much a part of our systems as pointing devices and keyboards.

There are clearly many areas that need additional work. Work to explore concurrency in multi-modal interfaces would be valuable. Currently, we are limited by tools, such as limitations of standard system components in accepting multiple input sources, in how easy it is to explore how different modes might be integrated so that people can talk, type and point at the same time and do so effectively in interacting with systems. We can imagine how pointing, combined with speech, might have helped solve some of our design problems, but we have not yet seen general purpose systems which do the integration well.

Do we see problems which may keep speech interfaces from becoming much more widely available in the future? Not really. Certainly, speech has some disadvantages for some situations (e.g., background noise) but so do keyboard (e.g., requires space) and pointing (e.g., relies on displays) modalities. There are some indications that speech input may interfere with other parallel cognitive activities more than typing, but at this point, it seems reasonable to expect that such impacts are minor. Would this go away with practice? We suspect it would, once HCI professionals have had the opportunity to spend as much effort to tune SUIs as the community has had to develop GUI designs.

### 2.2.1    FRAMING OUR ASR RESEARCH

We will talk about a range of research that we carried out across a period of time from 1992 to approximately 2000. It began with some early efforts to examine what was unique about the technology from a human perspective through the development of user interfaces for speech dictation (Karat, J., 1995; Danis and Karat, 1995) and picked up a few years after the introduction of IBM's large vocabulary speech recognition products (Karat et al. (1999); Halverson et al. (1999); Karat et al. (2000); and Cheng and Karat (2002)). The initial work is described first, followed by a discussion of later empirical work.

## 2.3    RESEARCH APPROACH AND TRADEOFFS

When we started working with ASR technology, it was clear that it was not yet mature. Even the researchers and developers of the technology were not using it in daily activities. Even so, we argued that in order to explore meeting users' needs, an examination of the real world task context was the proper "laboratory" for design research and application development. In such an environment, which we termed "technology-driven design" (Danis and Karat, 1995), we advocated leveraging niche markets to carry out early evaluations of technology use. By carefully selecting our users from areas where technology limitations were balanced by specific needs, we could develop applications that provided value. Additionally, we had long shared a belief in the emerging tenets of user-centered design (e.g., see Norman and Draper (1986)) and participatory design (see Muller and Kuhn (1993) for a discussion) with many of our colleagues in HCI. Happily, the importance of involving users from user groups targeted by the application is by now part of mainstream thought, as there is ample evidence of its benefits. Third, the potential of ASR technology to transform the work roles of its users requires that the individual, social and task contexts be addressed and brought into balance in the course of application development. Since it is impossible to replicate this multi-faceted environment within a laboratory, we felt that some of the design research must be situated in the context of actual work environments.

While in many ways the approach we take can be viewed as just another example of user-centered design in practice, we do feel that our dual focus of advancing the technology, while developing usable systems, provided a different focus to our approach than we might have if we were completely "user-centered." The domains we selected to work in and the interaction techniques we were willing to consider were colored by our specific interest of advancing a particular technology. This did not radically change our general approach to design (Karat, J., 1995), but it did influence factors we studied and the approach to design decisions we made.

## 2.3.1 WHY IS TECHNOLOGY-DRIVEN DESIGN NECESSARY?

We want to begin by offering a general description of "maturity" applied to HCI techniques. Mature HCI techniques can be thought of as those that have well understood technology bases and some general understanding concerning their domain of applicability. When described in this way, it should be clear that maturity is a relative rather than a binary term when describing HCI techniques. Without making too much of exactly where on a maturity scale various techniques would be, we would argue even in 2010 that keyboards and mice are relatively mature HCI techniques compared to speech or gesture recognition. The HCI community knows a fair amount about keyboard and mouse design, and it has developed many guidelines for use of these devices. It is important to distinguish between ASR as a technology (i.e., the algorithms and approaches for translating acoustic signals to text) and as a human-computer interaction technique (i.e., an approach to providing input to a system). A focus on ASR as an HCI technique requires that the technology be considered in the broader context of its ability to support task completion under a broad set of user contexts (e.g., deadlines, teamwork, etc.).

In order for ASR to function as a mature HCI technique, it must address such issues as recognition errors, variability in users' composition styles, the affordances of speech and the integration of multi-modal input. The solutions to these and other issues related to speech input constitutes a speech user interface (SUI), which will necessarily be strikingly different from today's graphical user interfaces (GUI). In the 1990's, we felt that our research could make a variety of contributions to evolving SUIs.

## 2.3.2 MATURING ASR TECHNOLOGY

Part of the reason that speech recognition could not be considered a mature HCI method derived from the fact that the technology itself was, and still is, evolving. One significant indicator was the lack of a general agreement about the capabilities of the technology. Performance characteristics for a mature technology can be expected to be well understood, and its design specifications should be well established. For example, the QWERTY keyboard design is an example of a mature technology. Its performance characteristics (e.g., typing speeds, error rates) have been established under a variety of describable situations and the same basic key organization has been stable even with the great change in physical realizations over the last century.

Performance characteristics are not well understood for ASR, the claims found in marketing literature for high accuracy notwithstanding. Marketing literature can be relevant to user experiences because it shapes the expectations of typical users. In reality, characterization of ASR performance is much more complex and can not be captured by a single number like recognition accuracy. The fact is that many factors affect recognition performance in ways that are not well understood, and that error correction is more complex than a casual consideration of it might suggest.

Research indicates that ASR performance varies as a function of task domain, match between task domain and dictated text, and speaker. The complexity of language usage (called a language model or LM) as reflected in the variety of word sequencing (a measure called perplexity) indicates that dictation in a domain such as radiology might be much easier for an ASR system than dictation in a domain such as journalism. The source of the difference derives from the fact that the recognition decision in any large vocabulary system in part depends on the ability of the language model to predict the sequence of words that the user will produce. Because the language used in radiology tends to be relatively stereotyped, it is easier to create a LM based on an analysis of radiology corpora that accurately reflects the language use of radiologists (Lai and Vergo, 1997). In an area such as journalism, the goal of text creation is often the creation of images in the readers' minds rather than simply communicating a set of facts. It is correspondingly more difficult to capture this type of language use in a LM through the techniques currently available. This sort of difference in domains led to research efforts to try and understand the user needs in each of them, and, subsequently, to the design ASR systems which addressed those needs. For radiology, constrained vocabularies and relatively consistent report styles contributed to LMs that produced accuracies which were high enough to result in product successes. For journalism, the commercial picture was less successful, though we would argue the lessons learned were more extensive.

Our early focus was not on trying to detail error rates or accurately measure dictation speeds. A central part of our argument to carry out use-based research was that it was unwise to wait until ASR technology was mature to build applications based on it. The problem with mature technology is that it is difficult and expensive to change. For example, consider the results of the various attempts to change keyboard layouts after people found possibly "better" ways to arrange the keys. A technology does, however, need to function reliably (i.e., does not crash regularly, delivers the specified functionality, is applicable to the chosen domain) in order for exploratory application research to begin. In addition, the technology has to be in a state where the basic problems have been solved, leaving the developers of the technology free to extend the technology by incorporating the functionality identified in research and development efforts, and to modify those aspects that do not work.

We identified several major issues that needed to be addressed in identifying the characteristics of a speech user interface. First, we felt there was a general lack of understanding in HCI approaches for how to address recognition technologies in which systems (rather than users) really can make mistakes. For speech recognition, there is a class of errors (called misrecognitions) in which the user speaks the intended word, but the system recognizes the word as something else. There is a tendency to consider the existence of misrecognitions to be an indication that the technology is immature, rather than accepting it as a defining characteristic of the technology. Error rates will decrease as basic ASR technology issues are successfully addressed, and improving ASR algorithms has been the lifelong pursuit of a number of researchers in our laboratory. However, recognition errors will always exist, if only because in a dictation task users will always use words which are not in the recognizer's vocabulary. The distinction between deterministic input technologies, such as a mouse and a keyboard, and technologies which have a probabilistic step interposed between the user action and the system response, such as ASR and handwriting recognition, is important. The appearance of errors in deterministic technologies is much easier for a user to understand and to avoid than arc errors that result in ASR. For example, if I type "ans" where I intended to type "and," I quickly come to the hypothesis that my finger accidentally hit a neighboring key, and I can resolve to be more precise in the future. However, the source of an error in speech recognition is much harder to diagnose. This is in part due to there being several factors that affect the output of the recognizer. Did I misspeak? Did I use a sequence of words that are unfamiliar to the system? Or was it an interaction of the two factors? Recognition errors can also do a great deal of damage to a user's documents; considerably more than can be caused with a keyboard. If, for example, a text word is misrecognized as a command, and this is not detected immediately by the user, a document can suffer serious damage if a command with an unrecoverable action is misrecognized. Thus, we consider designing for errors one of the most important tasks for designers of speech recognition systems.

Part of designing for errors includes developing methods of error correction which (1) help the system learn (i.e., eliminate repeated machine caused mistakes of that sort), (2) are well integrated into the task so that the user's attention is not consumed by the use of the technology but can remain on the task, and (3) are easy and fool-proof to execute (Rhyne and Wolf, 1993). We would argue that such techniques have evolved for keyboard and mouse interfaces, but they do not immediately extend to a SUI. Equally important is the development of alternative methods for manipulating the interface. While this is a generally agreed upon guideline in many interface systems, this is particularly important when working with HCI input techniques which are fallible. Speech as a viable HCI technique must also be able to accommodate the major text creation styles that people use.

Broadly, one can distinguish between writing in draft mode and writing by tinkering. In draft mode, writers enter a complete piece into the computer and begin editing only after all of the main thoughts have been captured. In contrast, a tinkering style combines what are separate text entry and editing stages in draft mode, so that the text is complete, except for fine tuning, as the writer moves down the piece. Reporters who participated in the StoryWriter project (Danis et al., 1994) tended to use a tinkering style. Such a style is very demanding for a speech-only interface because the user needs to move between a large vocabulary dictation task and small vocabulary command and control task rapidly and frequently. This research identified several problems which need to be solved to make this a smooth process, including the communication of mode switching information to the system with an easy and fail-safe method. Another critical component of an ASR-enabled interface is an understanding of the affordances of speech and to allow these to be combined with other input modalities. For example, in the StoryWriter project, which produced a low function editor for newspaper reporters suffering from repetitive stress injuries (RSI), researchers recommended use of a mouse for item selection combined with speech for specification of the action (Danis et al., 1994).

## 2.4    HCI RESEARCH RESULTS AND IMPACT

We turn now to some additional work which was carried out after the deployment of large vocabulary speech recognition systems by a number of vendors. In this work, we explicitly set out to better understand why this technology was not experiencing the rapid growth that had been expected. We found that a fairly common pattern was occurring in early adopters: products were purchased, used for a short period of time, and then abandoned. If the promise of the technology was true (i.e., "faster, easier, more natural text entry and system control"), why didn't everyone want one of these systems?

### 2.4.1   RESEARCHING TEXT CREATION AND ERROR CORRECTION WITH SPEECH RECOGNITION SYSTEMS

The research captured below summarizes research completed by our team in 1998 and 1999 (see Karat et al. (1999), and Halverson et al. (1999)). Looking back at this work, we are somewhat surprised that we were able to carry out such an extensive laboratory study in an industrial setting. It was an opportunity that we still remember fondly.

We were particularly interested in text creation by knowledge workers, defined as individuals who "solve problems and generate outputs largely by resort to structures internal to themselves rather than by resort to external rules or procedures" (Kidd, A., 1994). Text, in the form of reports or communication with others, is an important part of this output. While formal business communications used to pass through a handwritten stage before being committed to a typed document, this seemed to be becoming less frequent. Knowledge workers, who used to rely on secretarial help, are likely now to produce their own text by directly entering it into a word processor. During the time period of the research, however, a clear picture did not exist of how changes in the processes of text creation had impacted the quality of the resulting text.

ASR was clearly a promising technology for this task. We did not know how a change in modality of entry might impact the way in which people create text. For example, did voice entry affect the composition process? There is some suggestion that it does not impact composition quality (Gould et al., 1983; Ogozalek and Praag, 1986). Have people learned to view keyboards as "more natural" forms of communication with systems? While people can certainly dictate text faster than they can type, throughput with ASR systems appeared to be generally slower. We know now that productivity measures that include the time to make corrections favor keyboard-mouse input over speech, partially because error correction takes longer with speech. Some attempts have been made to address this in current systems, but the jury was still out on how successful such efforts might be at the time of this research.

Error detection and correction is an important arena in which to examine modality differences. For keyboard-mouse entry there are at least two ways in which someone might be viewed as making an error. One can mistype something by pressing one sequence of keys when one intended to enter another. Such user errors can be detected and corrected either immediately after they were made, within a few words of entry, during a proofreading of the text, or not at all. Another error is one of intent, and correcting this type of error requires editing the text as well. In both cases, correction can be made by backspacing and retyping, by selecting the incorrect text and retyping, or by dialog techniques generally available in word processing systems such as Find/Replace or Spell Checking.

While we do not have a clear picture of the proportion of use of the various techniques available, our observations suggest that all are used to some extent by experienced computer users.

There are some parallels for error correction in ASR systems. By monitoring the recognized text, users can correct misrecognitions with a speech command equivalent of backspacing. Current systems generally have several variations of a command that removes the most recently recognized text, such as "SCRATCH" or "UNDO." There are ways of selecting text. Generally, a user says the command "SELECT" and the string to be located, after which the user re-dictates to replace the selected text with newly recognized text. Additionally, correction dialogs provide users with a means of selecting a different choice from a list of possible alternatives or entering a correction by spelling it. These different correction mechanisms provide a range of techniques that map well to keyboard-mouse techniques. However, the field did not have evidence of how efficient or effective they were at that time. This study was designed to answer these questions. We were interested in several comparisons – keyboard and speech for text entry, modality effects on transcription and composition tasks, and error correction in different modalities.

### 2.4.2    SYSTEMS EVALUATED

Three commercially available large vocabulary continuous speech recognition systems were used in this study. All were shipped as products in 1998. These systems were IBM ViaVoice 98 Executive, Dragon Naturally Speaking Preferred 2.0, and L&H Voice Xpress Plus (referred to as IBM, Dragon and L&H below). While the products are all different in significant ways, they shared a number of important features. First, they all recognized continuous speech. Second, all had integrated command recognition into the dictation so that the user does not need to explicitly identify an utterance as text or command. In general, the systems provide the user with a command grammar (a list of specific command phrases), along with some mechanism for entering the commands as text. Commands can be entered as text by having the user alter the rate at which the phrase is dictated, pausing between words causes a phrase to be recognized as text rather than as a command.

While all of the systems function without specific training of a user's voice, we found the speaker independent recognition performance insufficiently accurate for the purposes of our study. To improve recognition performance, we had all users carry out speaker enrollment – the process of reading a body of text to the system and then having the system develop a speaker-specific speech model.

### 2.4.3    METHOD

There were different procedures used for the Initial Use and the Extended Use subjects in the study. Although the design of the Initial Use study was constructed to allow for statistical comparisons between the three systems, we reported on general patterns observed across the systems as they were of more general interest to the design of successful ASR systems. We collected both quantitative and qualitative data to assess user performance and satisfaction with the systems based on the completion of transcription and composition tasks. Efficiency in initial and repeated use of the systems was defined by time on task, text entry rate, and the number and type of errors. User satisfaction with the systems was measured through responses to questionnaires after task completion and through content analysis of qualitative data.

### 2.4.3.1   Initial Use

Subjects in the Initial Use study were 24 employees of IBM in the New York metropolitan area who were knowledge workers. While we do not consider this sample to be representative of the general population, we felt that it would provide us with a good basis for comparing the different systems. This is the sort of risk anyone involved in user research needs to evaluate. All the subjects were native English speakers and experienced computer users with good typing skills. Half of the subjects were male and half were female, with gender balanced across the conditions in the study. The age range of the subjects was from 20 to 55 years old. An effort was made to balance the ages of the subjects in the various conditions. Each subject was assigned to one of three speech recognition products, IBM, Dragon, or L&H. Half of the subjects completed text creation tasks (a mixture of dictation tasks and original composition tasks, both of which included proof-reading and error correction) using speech first and then did a similar set using keyboard-mouse, and half did keyboard-mouse followed by speech. Subjects received a $75 award for their participation in the three hour long session. All sessions were videotaped.

On arrival at the lab, the experimenter introduced the subject to the purpose, approximate length of time, and content of the usability session. The stages of the experimental session were the following:

1. Provide session overview and introduction.

2. Enroll user in assigned system.

3. Complete text tasks using first modality.

4. Complete text tasks using second modality.

5. Debrief the user.

The experimenter told the subject to try and complete the tasks using the product materials and to think aloud during the session. This required the subjects to indicate whether their speech was intended as system input or was directed somewhere else. While this could cause interference with the primary task, our subjects switched between think aloud (talking to the experimenters with the speech recognition microphone off) and task modes (talking to the system with the microphone on) fairly easily. The experimenter explained that assistance would be provided if the subject got stuck. The experimenter then left the subject and moved to the Control Room. The subject's first task was to enroll in the ASR system. The systems were pre-installed on the machines. Enrollment took from 30 minutes to 1.5 hours for the subject to complete, depending on the system and the subject's speed in reading the enrollment text. After enrollment was completed, the subject was given a break while the system developed a speech model for the subject by completing an analysis of the speech data. After the break, the subject attempted to complete a series of text creation tasks. All text was created in each product's dictation application that provided basic editing functions (similar to Windows 95 WordPad), and it did not include advanced functions such as spelling or grammar checkers.

Before engaging in the speech tasks, all participants underwent a training session with the experimenter present to provide instruction. This session was standardized across the three systems. Basic areas such as text entry and correction were covered. Each subject dictated a body of text supplied by the experimenter, composed a brief document, learned how to correct mistakes, and was given free time to explore the functions of the system. During the training session, each subject was shown how to make corrections as they went along as well as making corrections by completing dictation and going back and proofreading. Sample tasks in both transcription and composition were completed in this phase. Each subject was allowed approximately 40 minutes for the speech training scenario. Subjects were given no training for keyboard-mouse text creation tasks.

In the text creation phase for each modality, each subject attempted to complete four tasks - two composition and two transcription tasks. The order of the tasks (transcription or composition) was varied across subjects with half doing composition tasks followed by transcription tasks, and half doing transcription followed by composition. In all, each subject attempted to complete eight tasks, four compositions and four transcriptions, with two of each task type in each modality.

For each composition task, subjects were asked to compose a response to a message (provided on paper) in the simple text entry window of the dictation application. Each of the responses needed to contain three points for the reply to be considered complete and accurate. For example, in one of the composition tasks, the subject was asked to compose a message providing (1) a detailed meeting agenda, (2) meeting room location, and (3) arrangements for food. Composition tasks included social and work related responses, and subjects were asked to compose "short replies." The quality of each response was later evaluated based on whether the composed messages contained a complete and clear response that included information we deemed as important to the composition (e.g., the three points above for the meeting message) and was judged well written by evaluators. All subjects used the same four composition tasks, with an equal number of subjects using speech and keyboard-mouse to complete each task.

For transcription tasks, subjects attempted to complete the entry of two texts in each modality. There were four texts that ranged from 71 to 86 words in length. These texts were drawn from an old western novel because the text was written at a 5th grade level that was clear and simple to understand; enabled the extraction of short, meaningful, portions of text for the tasks; and the copyright on the book had expired (a key practical reason). The subjects entered the text in the appropriate modality and were asked to make all corrections necessary to match the content of the original text. The resulting texts were later evaluated for accuracy and completeness by comparing them to the original materials. Evaluators counted uncorrected entry errors and omissions.

In the keyboard-mouse modality tasks, subjects completed composition and transcription tasks using standard keyboard and mouse interaction techniques in a simple edit window provided with each system. Subjects were given 20 minutes to complete the four keyboard-mouse tasks. All subjects completed all tasks within the time limit.

In the speech modality tasks, subjects completed the composition and transcription tasks using voice, but were free to use keyboard and mouse for cursor movements or to make corrections they felt they could not make using speech commands. We intentionally did not restrict subjects to the use of speech to carry out the speech modality tasks, and all subjects made some use of the keyboard and mouse. Subjects were given 40 minutes to complete the four speech tasks.

After each of the tasks (enrollment and eight text tasks), subjects filled out a brief questionnaire on their experience completing the task. After completing the four tasks for each modality, subjects filled out a questionnaire addressing their experience with that modality. After completing all tasks, the experimenter joined the subject for a debriefing session in which the subject was asked a series of questions about their reactions to the ASR technology.

Why did we use such a wide range of measures in this study? This was primarily motivated by a desire to measure as much of the "user-experience" (a term not in general use in the 1990's) as possible. We did not have a specific theoretical perspective on the expected relationship between the measures, but we felt that "the more data the better" was an appropriate approach. Also, given the logistical requirements of the study (we knew any study would take a significant amount of time to complete), we wanted to capture as much as we could in one effort.

### 2.4.3.2  Extended Use

Subjects in the Extended Use study were the four researchers involved in the research project. In this study, each researcher used each of the three speech recognition products for 10 sessions of approximately one hour duration, a total of 30 sessions across the products. This duration was decided on during the planning stage for the project, and it was an amount of effort the team regarded as constituting more than just initial use. During the session, the researchers would use speech recognition software to carry out actual work related correspondence. After completing at least 20 sessions, the researchers completed the set of transcription tasks used in the Initial Use study.

The use of data from the researchers rather than recruiting external subjects was seen as the sort of compromise appropriate to industry research. As behavioral scientists, we were well trained not to trust self report data. However, we were also confronted with the logistical challenge of obtaining a sufficiently large sample of experienced user data. Various alternatives were considered (e.g., recruiting users of the various products), but in the end, we opted for the much easier approach of collecting data on ourselves. This was a risk – we were not entirely certain that the research community would accept such data as "unbiased" – particularly, if the IBM product was "best." We accepted the risk and imposed as much experimental rigor on the process as we could.

## 2.4.4    RESULTS

For the analysis of the Initial Use sessions, we carried out a detailed analysis of the videotapes of the experimental sessions. This included a coding of all of the pertinent actions carried out by subjects in the study. Misrecognitions of text and commands and attempts to recover from them were coded, along with a range of usability and system problems. Particular attention was paid to the interplay of text entry and correction segments during a task, as well as strategies used to make corrections. Because of the extensive time required to do this, we completed the detailed analysis for 12 of the 24 subjects in the Initial Use phase of the study (four randomly selected subjects from each of the three systems, maintaining gender balance). Thus, we report performance data from 12 subjects, but we include all 24 subjects in reporting results where possible. Additionally, we report selected data from the four subjects in the Extended Use phase. The data reported from the three speech recognition systems are collapsed into a single group here.

### 2.4.4.1    Typing Versus Dictating – Overall Efficiency

Our initial comparison of interest was the efficiency of text entry using speech and keyboard-mouse for transcription and composition tasks. We measured efficiency by time to complete the tasks and by entry rate. The entry rate that we presented was corrected words per minute (cwpm), and was the number of words in the final document divided by the time the subject took to enter the text and make corrections. The average length of the composed texts was not significantly different between the speech and keyboard-mouse tasks and was similar to the average length of the transcriptions (71.5 and 73.1 words for speech and keyboard-mouse compositions, respectively, and 77.8 words for transcriptions). Table 2.1 below summarizes the results for task completion rates for the various tasks.

| Table 2.1: Mean corrected words per minute and time per task by entry modality and task type in initial use (N=12). | | |
|---|---|---|
|  | Speech | Keyboard-mouse |
| Transcription | 13.6 cwpm | 32.5 cwpm |
|  | 7.52 min | 2.64 min |
| Composition | 7.8 cwpm | 19.0 cwpm |
|  | 9.96 min | 4.64 min |
| Average | 8.74 min | 3.64 min |

Creating text was significantly slower for the speech modality than for keyboard-mouse (F=29.2, p<0.01). By comparison, subjects in the Extended Use study completed the same transcription using ASR in an average 3.10 minutes (25.1 cwpm). The main effect for modality held for both the transcription tasks and the composition tasks. Composition tasks took longer than transcription tasks (F=18.6, p<0.01). This was to be expected given the inherent difference between simple text entry and crafting a message. There was no significant interaction between the task type and modality, suggesting that the modality effect was persistent across task type.

Given this clear difference in the overall time to complete the tasks, we were interested in looking for quantitative and qualitative differences in the performance. There are several areas in which we were interested in comparing text entry through typing to entry with ASR. These included the following: 1) number of errors detected and corrected in the two modalities, 2) differences in inline correction and proofreading as a means of correction, and 3) differences in overall quality of the resulting document. We consider evidence for each of these comparisons in turn.

### 2.4.4.2  Errors Detected and Corrected

A great deal of effort is put into lowering the error rates in ASR systems, in an attempt to approach the accuracy assumed for users' typing. For text entry into word processing systems, users commonly make errors (typing mistakes, misspellings and such) as they enter. Many of these errors are corrected as they go along – something that is supported by current word processing programs that highlight misspellings or grammatical errors. We were interested in data on the comparison of entry errors in the two modalities, and their detection and correction.

Table 2.2 presents data summarizing the average number of correction episodes for the different task types and input modalities. A correction episode was an effort to correct one or more words through actions that (1) identified the error and (2) corrected it. Thus, if a subject selected one or more words using a single select action and retyped or re-dictated a correction, we scored this as a correction episode. A major question was how the number of error correction episodes compared for ASR systems and keyboard-mouse entry.

Table 2.2:  Mean number of correction episodes per task by entry modality in initial use (N=12). Length in correction steps is in parentheses.

|  | Speech | Keyboard-mouse |
|---|---|---|
| Transcription | 11.3 (7.3) | 8.4 (2.2) |
| Composition | 13.5 (6.2) | 12.7 (2.4) |

While the average number of corrections made was slightly higher for the speech tasks than for the keyboard-mouse tasks, the length of the correction episodes was much longer. Interestingly, the improved performance for Extended Use subjects on transcription tasks could not be accounted for entirely by reduced correction episodes – subjects averaged 8.8 per task. The average number of steps per correction episode was much shorter for the Extended Use subjects – averaging 3.5 steps compared to 7.3 for Initial Use subjects.

In general, the keyboard corrections simply involved backspacing or moving the cursor to the point at which the error occurred, and then retyping (we coded these as a move step followed by a retype step). In a few instances, the user would mistype during correction, resulting in a second retype step. About 80% of the keyboard-mouse corrections were simple position/retype episodes.

For speech corrections there was much more variability. In most cases, a misrecognized word could be corrected using a simple locate/redictate command pair comparable to the keyboard-mouse pattern. Such a correction was coded as a voice move, followed by a voice redictate, that was marked to indicate success or failure. Variations include command substitutions such as the sequence voice select, voice delete, and voice redictate. More often the average number of commands required was much greater - generally, due to problems with the speech commands themselves that then needed to be corrected, although the overall patterns could still be seen in terms of moving to the error, selecting it and operating on it. Typical patterns were as follows:

1. Simple re-dictation failures in which the user selected the misrecognized word or phrase (usually using a voice select command), followed by a re-dictation of the misrecognized word which also was misrecognized. Users would continue to try to redictate, would use correction dialogs that allow for alternative selection or spelling, or would abandon speech as a correction mechanism and complete the correction using keyboard-mouse

2. Cascading failures in which a command used to attempt a correction was misrecognized and had to be corrected itself as a part of the correction episode. Such episodes proved very frustrating for subjects and took considerable time to recover from.

3. Difficulties using correction dialogs in which the user abandoned a correction attempt for a variety of reasons. This included difficulties brought on by mode differences in the correction dialog (e.g., commonly used correction commands such as "UNDO" would not work in correction dialogs) or difficulties with the spelling mechanism.

### 2.4.4.3  High Level Correction Strategies—Inline Versus Proofreading Corrections

Another question was whether users employ different correction strategies for the two input modalities. This could be demonstrated in either high-level strategies (such as "correct as you go along" versus "enter and then correct") or in lower-level differences such as the use of specific correction techniques. In Table 2.3, we presented data for the transcription and composition tasks combined, comparing the average number of errors corrected in a task before completion of text entry (Inline) and after reaching the end of the text (Proofreading).

Table 2.3: Average errors corrected per task by phase of entry in initial use (N=12).

|              | Speech | Keyboard-mouse |
|--------------|--------|----------------|
| Inline       | 8.6    | 8.8            |
| Proofreading | 4.2    | 1.6            |

There are two things to point out in these data. First, there were significantly more correction episodes in inline than in proofreading for both modalities (t=7.18, p<.006 for speech and t=8.64, p<.001 for keyboard-mouse). Performance on the keyboard-mouse tasks demonstrated that subjects were quite used to correcting as they go along, and the subjects tried to avoid separate proofreading passes. For the speech modality, however, subjects still had significant errors to correct in proofreading. In comparison, subjects in the Extended Use study rarely made inline corrections in transcription tasks, less than once per task on average.

Subjects gave us reasons for an increased reliance on proofreading. They commented that they felt aware of when they might have made a typing error, but felt less aware of when misrecognitions might have occurred. Note that in keyboard-mouse tasks, errors generally are user errors, while in speech tasks errors generally are system errors. By this we mean that for keyboard-mouse, systems reliably produce output consistent with user input. A typist can often "feel" or sense without looking at the display when an error might have occurred. For speech input, the user quickly learns that output is highly correlated with input, but that it is not perfect. Users do not seem to have a very reliable model of when an error might have occurred, and they must either constantly monitor the display for errors or rely more heavily on a proofreading pass to detect them.

Second, the number of inline correction episodes was nearly equal for the two conditions. This suggested a transfer of cognitive skill from the more familiar keyboard and mouse interaction. As in typing, subjects were willing to switch from input mode to correction mode fairly easily and did not try to rely completely on proofreading for error correction.

### 2.4.4.4  Lower-Level Strategies for Error Correction

Almost all keyboard-mouse corrections were made inline and simply involved using the backspace key or mouse to point and select followed by typing. In comparison, the voice corrections were much more varied. This is undoubtedly due to the wide range of possible errors in the ASR systems compared to keyboard-mouse entry. There are major classes of possible errors in ASR:

**Simple misrecognitions** in which a single spoken word intended as text is recognized as a different text word.

**Multi-word misrecognitions** in which a series of words are recognized as a different series of words.

**Command misrecognitions** in which an utterance intended as a command is inserted in the text.

**Dictation as command misrecognitions** in which an utterance intended as dictation is taken as a command.

All of these occurred in all of the systems in the study. In addition, subjects did some editing of content in their documents. Because errors in ASR are correctly spelled words, it is difficult to separate edits from errors in all cases. In what follows, these were treated the same since both use the same techniques for correction.

Methods of making corrections in the two modalities could be compared. For example, keyboard-mouse corrections could be made by making a selection with the mouse and then retyping, by positioning the insertion point with cursor keys and then deleting errors and retyping, or by simply backspacing and retyping. These segments fell into two categories: deleting first then entering text or selecting text and entering over the selection. In speech, these kinds of corrections were possible in a variety of ways using re-dictation after positioning (with voice, keyboard or mouse). In addition, there was use of a correction dialog which allowed spelling (all systems) or selection of an alternative word (in two of the three systems). Table 2.4 summarizes the techniques used by subjects to make corrections in the texts.

| Table 2.4: Patterns of Error Correction based on overall corrections in initial use (N=12). | | |
|---|---|---|
| | **Speech** | **Keyboard-mouse** |
| **Select** text then reenter | 38% | 27% |
| **Delete** then reenter | 23% | 73% |
| Correction box | 8% | NA |
| Correcting problems caused during correction | 32% | NA |

The dominant technique for keyboard entry was to erase text back to the error and retype. This included the erasure of text that was correct, and reentering it. For speech, the dominant technique was to select the text in error and to redictate. In only a minority of the corrections (8%) did the subjects utilize the systems' correction dialog box. Almost a third of the corrections were to correct problems created during the original correction attempt. For example, while correcting the word "kiss" to "keep" in "kiss the dog", the command "SELECT kiss" is misrecognized as the dictated text "selected kiss," which must be deleted in addition to correcting the original error.

Low use of the correction dialogs might be explained by two phenomena. First, correction dialogs were generally used after other methods had failed (62% of all correction dialogs). Second, 38% of the time a problem occurred during the interaction inside the correction dialog with 38% of these resulting in canceling out of the dialog. Understanding more fully why the features of the correction dialogs are not better utilized was considered an area for future study.

### 2.4.4.5  Overall Quality of Typed and Dictated Texts

There were two areas in which we tried to evaluate the relative quality of the results of text entry in the two modalities. For transcription tasks, we evaluated the overall accuracy of the transcriptions – that is, we asked how many mismatches there were between the target document and the produced document. For composition tasks, we asked three peers, not part of the study, to evaluate several aspects of the messages produced by subjects. These judges independently counted the number of points that the message covered (there were three target points for each message). We also asked for a count of errors in the final message and for an evaluation of the overall clarity. Finally, for each of the four composition tasks, we asked the judges to rank order the 24 messages in terms of quality from best to worst.

In Table 2.5, we summarized the overall quality measures for the texts produced. These measures included average number of errors in the final products for both the transcription and composition tasks and the average quality rank for texts scored by three judges for the composition tasks.

**Table 2.5:** Mean quality measures by modality in initial use (N=24).

|                      | Speech      | Keyboard-mouse |
| -------------------- | ----------- | -------------- |
| Transcription errors | 3.8 errors  | 1.0 errors     |
| Composition errors   | 1.8 errors  | 1.1 errors     |
| Composition (rank)   | 13.2        | 11.4           |

There were many more errors in the final transcription documents for the speech tasks than for the keyboard-mouse tasks. The errors remaining in the final documents were broken into three categories: wrong words (including misspellings), format errors (including capitalization and punctuation errors), and missing words. The average number of wrong words (F=25.4, p<.001) and format errors (F=12.6, p<.001) were significantly lower for keyboard-mouse compared with speech tasks. There was no difference in the number of missing words.

Composition quality showed a similar pattern. Errors in composition included obviously wrong words (e.g., grammar errors) or misspellings. There were fewer errors in the keyboard-mouse texts than in the speech texts (F=7.9, p<0.01). Judges were asked to rank order the texts for each of the four composition tasks from best (given a score of 1) to worst (given a score of 24). While the mean score was lower (better) for keyboard-mouse texts than for speech texts, the difference was not statistically significant.

### 2.4.4.6  Transcription Versus Composition

For both the keyboard-mouse modality and the speech modality, composition tasks took longer than transcription tasks. We did not find significant differences in the length or readability of texts composed in the two modalities. Additionally, topics such as correction techniques or error frequencies did not seem to vary between modalities and task types.

### Subjective Results – Questionnaire Data

Subjects (N=24) in the Initial Use study consistently reported being dissatisfied with the ASR software for performing the experimental tasks. When asked to compare their productivity using the two modalities in the debriefing session, subjects gave a modal response of "much less productive" for speech on a 7-point scale ranging from "much more productive" to "much less productive," and 21 of 24 subjects responded "less" or "much less productive." Subjects' top reasons for their ratings, with frequency of response in parentheses summed across several questions:

- Speech recognition is unreliable, error prone (34).

- Error correction in speech is much too hard – and correction can just lead to more errors (20).

- Not knowing how to integrate the use of speech and keyboard-mouse efficiently (19).

- Keyboard is much faster (14).

- Command language problems (13).

- It is harder to talk and think than to type and think (7).

Additionally, when asked if the software was good enough to purchase, 21 of 24 subjects responded "No" to a binary Yes/No choice. The three subjects that reported a willingness to purchase the software all gave considerable qualifications to their responses. When asked for the improvements that would be necessary for ASR technology to be useful, subjects' top responses included:

- Corrections need to be much easier to make (27).

- Speech recognition needs to be more accurate (25).

- Need feedback to know when there is a mistake (8).

- Command language confusion between command and dictation needs to be fixed (8).

## 2.4.5   CONCLUSIONS

It is interesting to note that several of the Initial Use subjects commented that keyboard entry seemed "much more natural" than speech for entering text. While this seems like an odd comment at some level, it reflected the degree to which some people have become accustomed to using keyboards. This relates both to the comfort with which people compose text at a keyboard and to well learned methods for inline error detection and correction. Speech is also a well learned skill, though as this study shows, the ways to use it in communicating with computers are not well established for most users. There is potential for ASR to be an efficient text creation technique – the Extended Use subjects entered transcription text at an average rate of 107 uncorrected words per minute – however, correction took them over three times as long as entry time on average.

When desktop ASR systems first began appearing in the mid 1990's, it was assumed that their wide-scale acceptance would have to await solutions to "mode problems," that is, the need to explicitly indicate dictation or command modes, and the development of continuous speech recognition algorithms which were sufficiently accurate. While all of the commercial systems evaluated in this study had these features, our results indicated that our technically sophisticated subject pool was far from satisfied with the systems as an alternative to keyboard for general text creation. They gave a clear prioritization of changes needed in the design of these systems. In 2010, these changes still merit significant attention. We take this as evidence that more research still need to be done – both in developing the technology itself and in exploring ways to make it more usable. While the technology seems acceptable for some populations (RSI sufferers or technology adopters), wide scale acceptance still awaits design improvements beyond this current generation of products.

## 2.5    LESSONS LEARNED FROM THE HCI RESEARCH

We generally consider technology-driven design as involving the dual mission of advancing technology and supporting user work. Our intent in looking for applications to work on is not just to look for ways in which information technology can provide value in the work context but specifically to look for applications which might be well suited to the particular hammer that we are wielding (ASR in this case). Good candidates for technology-driven design then are those in which the technology can really provide useful benefits and that also offer challenges to the techniques under consideration. We acknowledge the limitations we placed ourselves under in doing this, but we felt that advancing ASR as an HCI technique was a valuable goal for future information technology systems. We did not hesitate in letting those we worked with know that working with and gaining a better understanding the ASR technology, its usefulness, and potential application was part of our project goal.

What was our ASR experience? Attempts to introduce new technology into the workplace can fail for so many reasons that we feel it is particularly important to take considerable care with projects in which the technology itself is not mature. There is a tendency to blame the technology as the reason for such failures and prematurely dismiss it, rather than trying to build on early experiences. We believe that our explicit admission that we want to make use of immature technology in a project helped keep the expectations of all parties realistic. We do, however, think that it is important to select applications in which you have a strong reason to expect that the technology can provide users with real benefits.

Involvement with the development of ASR technology has given us the opportunity to develop an understanding of some of the things to look for identifying good candidate domains for early use of speech recognition interfaces. Careful screening of potential customers by attending to the domain and the individuals and organization that the HCI expert will be working with is necessary since development of a system with ASR can require considerable creativity in places where development with mature techniques can more easily rely on known solutions. Again, the ease of error correction is a good example. There were not at that time, and to a large extent are still not, generally accepted techniques for handling the various consequences of the fact that user input can be misrecognized by ASR systems.

Technology-driven design projects involve a fairly high risk. Being a part of the maturation of new techniques and technologies is not for everyone or every context. For many reasons, some organizations and contexts will be more receptive as contexts for relatively early technology projects. There are a number of factors that we have found to be important in the process of targeting 'an application area and establishing a relationship with a customer.' There are some general factors:

**Development for a specific customer with their involvement.** Part of the targeting decision needs to ensure that both the customer and the members of the development team are willing to view the project as a joint effort. This requires an effort on the part of the technology provider to resist the temptation to limit communication with the customer once a project has been started and an effort on the part of the customer to resist thinking that the technology developer can produce the desired result without continually trying to communicate what that result might be. Another way of viewing this is to say that HCI experts need to make sure that all parties are willing to take part in a participatory design project in which both acknowledge the interests of the other. You need to be clear in such projects that the HCI interests go beyond traditional "payments for services" that usually cover the interests of the development organization.

**Commitment from partner to use systems as they become available, even if not stable.** In most relationships where there is a customer and a provider, the customer would prefer to know when the finished (defect free) system will be delivered and does not want to be a part of evaluating the preliminary (buggy) systems. For immature HCI techniques, both parties must be willing to tolerate the expectations of the other. At the same time, we need to be able to provide reasonable assurances to the customer that real work carried out with preliminary systems will not be wasted (i.e., we need to keep from requiring the user to duplicate work). Through the years, we have met customers who have strategic planning groups with information technology visionaries who are eager to try the emerging technologies. These people see it as a competitive advantage to learn about new tools which are still under development. Careful recruitment of customers to collaborate with is essential for success in this type of research project. For those who perceive the benefits of early experience with new technology as outweighing the costs of disruption in current practices, it can be a win-win situation.

**Education of partner about the technology and how it affects them.** Everyone, both on the technology provider side and on the customer side, will underestimate the impacts of new technology. Techniques such as ASR will redefine many tasks and jobs. For example, introduction of speech recognition technology might impact how offices are laid out or how someone "makes notes" while in front of a client. Again, with a set of customer representatives who have the skills to think strategically or in visionary ways, and who have deep expertise in their business domains, these interactions can be very fruitful and the education and insights occur for all parties involved in the project.

## 2.5.1    ISSUES IN RESEARCH IMPACTING THE DEVELOPMENT PROCESS

Selection of an appropriate client and domain is only the first part of the effort. What remains is the hard work of participatory design with "use of ASR" as a constraint. Since all designs are done within a context of constraints, adding of this one does not change the remaining process in any fundamental way. The immaturity of the interface technique served to raise our awareness of the importance of some of the techniques of usability engineering and participatory design, and we have found that we rely particularly on the following:

- Task analysis and early user input. Since potential users generally have no experience with the technique, you can not rely on accumulated experience of HCI studies to inform design for the given context. We must become domain-knowledgeable and continually review the design direction with the users.

- Use of early prototypes. The naturalness of speech is both a feature and a curse in that users have expectations about the look and feel of interacting through voice, but they are fairly blind to the subtle ways in which communicating through voice with a machine will be different than with a human. Prototypes of all levels of fidelity, from paper mock-ups to early releases of fully-enabled systems, must be examined in simulated use. For example, we created story board mockups of error correction techniques for exploration with developers during the design of the IBM technology.

- Anticipating work context impacts. HCI researchers need to prepare the organization for the use of the ASR-enabled application. This includes education of the individuals and the organization about what to expect from the system and what not to expect. As much as possible, we try to keep from creating extra work for the early prototype users (e.g., by having the work they do with the system converted into real work output).

- Designing for errors. Errors with recognition technologies are more varied and complex than errors with direct response technologies such as keyboards and pointing devices. Because the HCI field does not have a well developed understanding of when these will occur and how to accommodate them, this aspect of design requires special attention throughout development.

There is a relationship with one more party in the research that bears mentioning here. For our work in speech recognition, the research group responsible for development of the technology – the speech recognition algorithms group – was a very interested party. This group had a long history of innovation in the ASR field, and the group was eager to find out the results of our investigations into the usefulness of the technology. This was particularly true since there were systems comparisons in an area where competitive claims of superiority were seen as important to product success. On one hand, we needed to take precautions to ensure objectivity. We knew the research results would be questioned if we found the IBM system to be superior. On the other, we needed to ensure that our results could be seen as valuable to the field even if they did not show superiority of our own systems. In the end, much to their credit, the IBM speech recognition team was satisfied that we had done a good job even though they did not "win." If the results of the comparative study had been significantly different, the path to making our results "vital to the corporation" might have been different, but we believe there still would have been important research results. We view time spent anticipating different research outcomes while planning such projects as an important activity.

CHAPTER 3

# Case Study 2: Personalization in eCommerce

## 3.1 BACKGROUND ON THE DOMAIN OF STUDY

Personalizing a user experience means making use of personal data in a business context to provide value to the customer and the business. Personalization builds on privacy, security, and trust in the context of the user task. Information about a user can be either explicitly gathered or implicitly obtained. We define the use of information about a user to alter the content and functionality of the user experience *Personalizing Interaction*. While there has been a fair amount of research aimed at enabling systems to tailor interaction based on some understanding of the user, prior work has examined fairly narrow contexts. Examples of this research on techniques or methods to infer user goals include click-stream analysis (Barrett et al., 1997), collaborative filtering (Burke, R., 1999; Schafer et al., 1999; Schonberg et al., 2000), and data mining of web user logs (Heer and Chi, 2002; Mobasher et al., 2000; Perkowitz and Etzioni, 2000; Spiliopoulou, M., 2000). Newer techniques include using pattern classification and developing recommender systems (Duda et al., 2001; Resnick and Varian, 1997), combining historical profile data and online visitation patterns (VanderMeer et al., 2000) and online heuristic decision-making based on flowchart and rule-based constructs (Anupam et al., 2001).

In general, these methods attempt to predict user interests or goals and automatically personalize or adapt the presentation of information. Traditionally, most interactions with computers take place between a system that understands little of the particular user (i.e., they have no or a very limited user model) and individuals who have limited understanding of the system or application (i.e., they have a limited conceptual model of the system). Over the last few decades, the general population has developed more sophisticated conceptual models of the technology they use, while the technology demonstrates relatively small advances in understanding the humans they serve.

We view a future in which human-computer interaction is greatly enhanced through advances in the ability of technology to employ personal information about users to realize better, more valuable interactions for users and providers alike. Although computer systems are often seen as entities in and of themselves, in e-commerce and many other domains, they are really a set of tools which facilitate business transactions. This research began to provide a better understanding of the context in which users provide various kinds of information to systems so that the systems can provide value to the interaction between humans who communicate and interact with each other through the technology.

### 3.1.1   FRAMING PERSONALIZATION

We define *personalizing a website* to mean using personal information about an individual to tailor the experience for that individual on the site. We consider personal information as including a very broad range of elements - from basic identifying information such as age and income to information we are just beginning to be able to collect such as intention or emotional state. We will use the terms "personalize" and "personalization" here primarily because these terms are most commonly used in current Web applications and research. The terms "adaptive," "context-aware," and "tailored experience" have also been used to describe the elements we are addressing. Further, we define a *personalization policy* as a decision made by an e-commerce company involving the handling of personal data on the company's website. A *personalization feature* is a method for collecting and using personal information in order to tailor a website visitor's experience on the website. A personalization policy applies to the whole website, while a feature provides functionality for a particular task on the site. Examples of personalization policies include the degree of visibility and control over personal data that is given to website visitors. Examples of personalization features include collaborative filtering and adaptive navigation.

We view personalization for e-commerce as involving an exchange between at least two parties. In general, there are two roles in the interaction - that of **customer** and that of **provider** of the product or service. Any interaction, in which information about the parties involved is used to adapt the interaction, can be said to be "personalized."

Second, we believe the essential goal of personalization is to provide increased value to both parties though the use of personal information (Godin, S., 1999; Peppers and Rogers, 1997). Most research to date has focused on personalization as involving just the user (customer) of a system. The basic model is that a person divulges information in return for some promised benefit. This exchange can be viewed as involving a value proposition in which the value to the customer is a function of the costs of divulging information and the perceived benefits of doing so. We extend this notion of a value proposition for personalization to include consideration of the provider's value proposition - that is, the value of any personalization feature to the organization responsible for developing the system is a function of the cost of implementation and the benefits obtained from doing it. Thus, for the Customer, the value of personalization = f (cost of divulging, perceived benefits) and for the Provider, value is a function of (cost of gathering information, perceived value). For the Provider's Value Proposition (PVP), costs and benefits can generally be transformed into monetary units. For the Customer's Value Proposition (CVP), costs and benefits are more complex, and can involve other factors.

Specifically, we suggest that the costs and benefits must be viewed within a framework of human values that extends beyond simple economic benefit and includes concepts of security, privacy, trust, and business relationships. For example, to go one level deeper in our framework, we view Customer Cost for a personalization feature to be a function of the information requirements of the feature (e.g., explicit or implicit information), the context of the interaction (e.g., for one-time visit or long-term relationship), customer trust in the provider (e.g., well known or new contact), privacy (how much control does the user have over access to and use of their personal information), and personal predispositions to divulge information (e.g., no fear or generally wary).

### 3.1.2    THE PERSONALIZATION VALUE SPACE

When we talk about personalization, we assume we are addressing a whole range of information types and possible values to customers and businesses. For example, various projects within IBM Research are aimed at "knowing the user" on an individual level and as a member of some category of users (e.g., expert web user). These efforts include everything from identifying product preferences (through explicit questions), to inferring current goal intention (through gaze or click stream), to attempting to identify emotional state (though facial expression). Technologies vary in computational complexity, including various rule engines or user model based calculations. Our research was not aimed specifically at identifying a single "best technique." We do not believe this is a reasonable goal because our work suggests that (1) the value of techniques to any customer will vary with the role of the customer at any given time, (2) the value of a technique to a business will depend on the kind of business objectives they have, and (3) there are likely to be interactions between techniques resulting in a package of techniques that would be optimally effective.

Our research explored this Personalization Value Space (PVS) through an examination of personalization policies (e.g., permission marketing, levels of identity), feature categories (e.g., collaborative filtering, click stream analysis), user characteristics (e.g., predisposition to trust, interaction goal), and business context (e.g., product offering, business goals). We believe that the effectiveness of personalization efforts are a function of these four components (i.e., Effectiveness = f (policy, feature, user context, business context)).

This conception of personalization does not stand alone; we view personalization as closely tied to Privacy and Security research. While Privacy deals essentially with users controls over information about themselves, personalization is concerned with the value that might be realized by a customer and provider from sharing information with one another. In general, Security research has to do with the confidence that data can not be compromised or taken by unauthorized sources. We believe that both Customers and Providers view security as essential to proceeding with any interaction between them. Extending this, we view Trust as an important element of the value propositions for both customers and providers in any interaction. Customer trust of an e-business develops through their perception that the data they provide is secure, will be used only as they allow, and provides them value.

## 3.2    PURPOSE OF THE HCI RESEARCH

The goals of this HCI research project were 1) to understand the value of personalization to customers and IBM and 2) to develop the strategy for bringing personalization to the ibm.com public web site which ensures that the top-priority goals of customers and the business are met. The ibm.com site in 2003 included 4 million pages of content on 2,200 sub sites. In consultation with business executives, we decided to limit the scope of our research on personalization of the ibm.com site to the content areas related to servers and personal computer information, sales, and support. We also integrated our activities with related human-computer interaction (HCI) efforts on the site. The multidisciplinary team of five researchers had eight months in 2003 to complete the work, and we collaborated with several groups across IBM to accomplish the goals.

## 3.3   RESEARCH APPROACH AND TRADEOFFS

The project team followed IBM's User-Centered Design process to complete the major set of activities and deliverables for the project (Vredenburg et al., 2001). We made a number of decisions about how best to use the 8-month period of time we had been given to complete the research. We also believed that understanding our stakeholders' view of the domain was critical to the success of the research and allocated sufficient time for the HCI interviews and observations to identify key business requirements. To enable the team to have the most productive sessions possible with the stakeholders, we believed that completing a literature review was an essential and efficient way to ramp up on the identified user requirements and design options as explored in the public domain. Being part of a large organization, we were able to leverage the expertise of other researchers around the world through brainstorming sessions which were rapid and valuable means of building on the work and expertise of others within the organization.

Completing these activities somewhat in parallel provided the opportunity for valuable cross-pollination, as well as iterative work in the completion of these initial activities. In terms of tradeoffs, direct communication with a sponsor of your research is not an area to compromise on. You must have the opportunity to discuss with the sponsor and/or stakeholder the business reason for the HCI research. The business reason for the research must be clear or there is little chance for success from the outset.

We knew from past experience about the amount of time to allocate to the iterative user studies that were a central part of the research, as well as the time needed to reflect on the results and create the deliverables. Also, based on communication through our social network within the organization, we learned about a couple of internal marketing and usability research studies on closely related topics that we were able to join in the planning stages, add content related to the personalization research to, and were then able to participate onsite with the other researchers in the data collection activities with the usability study participants. Direct work with users is also an area that must not be compromised.

There are many tradeoffs that can be made in terms of how you work with users, in what type of user study is conducted, but there is no substitute for direct access to the target users of the system you are conducting the HCI research on. Ideally, a good mix of field and laboratory user studies would be best, and please see Mayhew's book on the usability lifecycle (Mayhew, D., 1999) or a summary by our team (Karat et al., 2005) for a description of the different HCI activities to conduct during each stage of research and development. However, in the real world, there is rarely time, resource, and expertise to do the research you would like to do. So, the best solution is often to define a mix of adapted versions of HCI activities that enable you and your team, in the time allocated, to understand and design for the user, the user's tasks, and context of use for the system under study, so that there is an expectation that you have allowed yourselves the possibility to identify the best, most efficient and effective solution given the constraints, and you have eliminated all significant sources of risk.

We provide an overview of the major HCI activities and the initial results that shaped the iterative user studies covered later in the case study (see Figure 3.1). The components in the figure will be discussed shortly. Just for context though, please understand that column one represented our research to understand the problem space, column two covered research to create the base strategy and master list of features to apply to the V11/V12 PCD and Servers content area on the site that our team was asked to focus the personalization research on, column three represents the three iterations of design and testing that were completed with users during which significant improvement occurred, and column four represents the results of our analysis of the user performance and satisfaction data and the resulting deliverables.

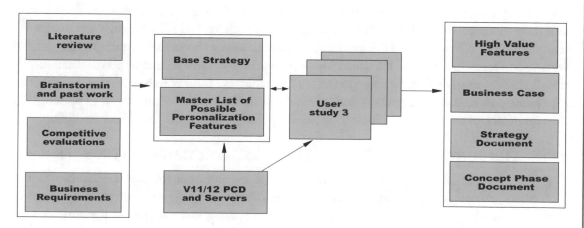

Figure 3.1: Major HCI activities in personalization research.

In terms of the allocation of time across the activities in Figure 3.1, the team worked on the first column of activities, which resulted in the second column of initial deliverables, about 2.5 months; the iteration of three user studies, including the design of all study materials, the recruitment of participants by a third-party vendor using a participant profile we created, and data analysis, consumed about 4.5 months, and the deliverables listed in the last column were completed in the last month, and then presented and discussed during several different meetings with the sponsors.

Each HCI research activity was allocated a target amount of time in the schedule, with some flexibility built into the schedule. We have learned over time the value of scoping the activity to fit comfortably within target ranges, as external events will occur that require time and resource to address. Some of these unanticipated events, such as learning about other related studies where we could collaborate with other researchers and accomplish much more than we could simply within our own team, had very positive results for the research. If you have left yourself no flexibility in your commitments and schedule though, you can not take advantage of these opportunities. Similarly, when the prototype, which we had tested, failed in one of the user sessions, and we had to reschedule participants, we used some of the flexibility in the schedule. Other 'grace periods' were used to handle no-shows by participants, although these events are expected and are routinely built into the schedule as a matter of best practice in the field.

### 3.3.1   LITERATURE REVIEW AND BRAINSTORMING SESSIONS REGARDING PERSONALIZATION IN E-COMMERCE

We began the project by completing a literature review of the published research in the area of personalization. We conducted the review to identify possible personalization features and to understand the state of the art. The review covered the personalization literature, e-commerce research and literature including one-to-one marketing and permission marketing, adaptive hypermedia literature, and review of confidential internal personalization, e-commerce, and HCI research and market intelligence reports. We enriched this summary of information by conducting a brainstorming session with IBM researchers around the world who were working in areas related to personalization. We stated our project goals and requested ideas for personalization features to be considered in the concept phase user studies with customers who would experience interactive prototypes of personalized user interfaces to the site. At this point, we did not prejudge techniques for lack of feasibility.

### 3.3.2   HEURISTIC USABILITY EVALUATIONS OF COMPETITIVE SITES

The team completed a set of heuristic evaluations of the ibm.com site and key competitors to understand current best practices regarding the user experience of personalization in e-commerce sites, to expand our feature list, assess IBM's competitiveness, and understand opportunities for leadership. We reviewed the Dell, Hewlett Packard, Compaq, IBM, Sun and Amazon sites using a set of six typical task scenarios covering the purchase and support of computer hardware and accessories. Each of the team members was randomly assigned to conduct heuristic reviews using a subset of the six user task scenarios on a subset of the six sites. Team members took on the roles of the typical users of the sites, completed the task scenarios, and recorded qualitative and qualitative data on their experiences. The results of the competitive heuristic analysis of the six sites showed that most sites were in their infancy with regard to personalization with the obvious exception of Amazon. Many sites had extremely cumbersome and fractured user experiences. The review generated a list of 18 initial design recommendations that were incorporated into both the base strategy as hypotheses and the master list of possible personalization features.

### 3.3.3   BUSINESS REQUIREMENTS IDENTIFICATION

The team employed an adaptation of contextual inquiry methods (Beyer and Holtzblatt, 1998) to identify the business requirements of ibm.com stakeholders regarding personalization of the site and the underlying value model of personalization. Contextual inquiry is an HCI method that enables practitioners to identify user issues through observation of users in context, use of probing questions, and collection and analysis of key data points. Inductive reasoning is employed to identify issues through the "voice of the customer" and build hierarchies from the bottom up based on data instances, to a larger view of patterns, and affinity diagrams of the associations that highlight common issues and themes of customer issues and requirements.

The ibm.com stakeholders were the primary user group to identify business requirements. We adapted contextual inquiry methods to the area of business requirements identification. We combined the use of probing questions with user observation to gain a deep understanding of stakeholder goals through analysis of key data points and the construction of affinity diagrams and the model of personalization from them. We met with 12 representatives of marketing, sales, development, finance, solutions, support, and hardware and software brands. Teams of two met with each stakeholder and sometimes his or her associate. We asked them to tell us about the business goals they were responsible for related to the site and potential personalization of it. We probed for specific examples of statements to ground them in real events. We observed each user work environment for a maximum of 120 minutes.

The resulting affinity diagrams document the stakeholders' business requirements regarding customer experience goals for the site, the quality of customer relationships, business financial goals, and infrastructure goals for the site. The analysis also identified the target customers of personalization, themes regarding the personalization pilot on the site, and identification of obstacles and limitations in achieving the identified goals. With these data, we built the business view of the Value Model of Personalization and combined it with the customer view obtained during the user studies to complete the personalization value model discussed later in this paper.

### 3.3.4   THE MASTER LIST OF POSSIBLE PERSONALIZATION FEATURES

The team gathered information from as many sources as possible about potential personalization features that might be used to provide value to customers and the business on the ibm.com site. Space prohibits us from providing the complete list here; however, there were 75 personalization features that we initially catalogued, and we view this list as a snapshot in time. The list will evolve and change across time. We present a summary of the general clusters into which the personalization polices and features appeared in Table 3.1 below.

Our goal was to study as wide a range of personalization features as possible. However, we hypothesized that having a central place on the website around which all the personalization features could be accessed and all personal data found would be seen as valuable to website visitors. We choose to use the construct of a *Personal Book*, created by Dr. Clare-Marie Karat in previous e-commerce research (Berreby, D., 1999), to test this hypothesis. The Personal Book, referenced in the first cluster in Table 3.1, is a personal space on the website which is created when a visitor chooses to register with the site. It is available from any page within the site and provides the visitor with both constant access to his or her profile and quick links to all of the other personalization features, such as a

**Table 3.1:** Personalization feature clusters.

| |
|---|
| Personal book (portal), where all personal data can be accessed and modified |
| Universal profile or one account for the entire site |
| Subscription-based services |
| Service and support |
| Recommendations based on profile data |
| Adaptive presentation tailored to user characteristics |
| Personal preferences in page layout or format (customization) |
| Adaptive navigation |
| Live chat-like or phone-based help or sales support (personal shopper) |
| Feedback that system recognizes a "repeat" visitor |
| Transaction history |
| Loyalty programs, incentives |
| Future purchase considerations |
| Your store, built by an expert |

list of purchased products that allows users to track transactions, find compatible accessories, find replacements for discontinued items, and see a history of their IT purchases. Figure 3.2 shows an illustration of the Personal Book used in the Study 3 prototype. Other personalization features available through the Personal Book include the ability to filter products based on user needs and the ability to indicate items that the user may wish to purchase in the future so that they are notified of special offerings involving those products.

In addition, there were three personalization policies that we hypothesized were crucial to the success of personalization on the site and that formed the base strategy. They were: 1) giving website visitors control of the data in their profiles, 2) asking visitors for the minimal amount of personal information necessary and providing immediate value to the customer based on use of it (Permission Marketing), and 3) enabling website visitors to adopt different levels of identity as appropriate to their tasks on the website. Each of these will be discussed in more detail below.

## 3.3.5   OWNERSHIP OF DATA

In the past, many companies viewed the data they collected about visitors to their website as something the company owned and could use in any way it liked. This view has been changing for some time. Both social and legal pressures in Europe have forced companies to view personal data as being owned by the subject of the data (Kobsa, A., 2002). The United States has been slower to adopt laws, preferring to have business self-regulate; however, similar pressures are at work (Arent Fox, 2003; Volokh, E., 2000). Given this trend, we wanted to explicitly include the policy that customers own their own data to understand its value to e-commerce customers. By "own their own data," we

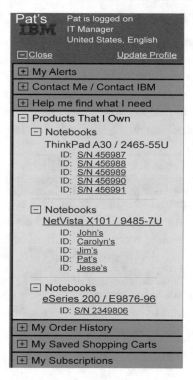

**Figure 3.2:**  Design of the Personal Book.

mean, customers can view, edit, and delete information about themselves, their purchases, and their actions on the website at any point in time and give permission for the e-commerce company for specific uses of the data.

## 3.3.6    PERMISSION MARKETING

Permission Marketing (Godin, S., 1999) is the concept that a customer's profile is built slowly over time as the individual develops trust in the e-commerce company. The customer is only asked to provide the information needed to enable specific services and receives immediate value for all the information that he or she provides. Many personalized websites at the time of the study required that anyone who wanted to use any personalization features on the site had to register by filling out lengthy questionnaires. Hagan found that people often defeat the purpose of these forms by entering incorrect information (Hagen, P., 2000). We wanted to determine if only asking for the information needed to provide an immediate service to website users would increase their willingness to share data.

### 3.3.7  LEVELS OF IDENTITY ON AN E-COMMERCE WEBSITE

Schaffer defines the levels of identity concept as the degree of personal information to which a website has access based on the type of relationship between the e-commerce company and the customer at any given point in time (Schaffer, J., 2001). According to Schaffer's definition, this ranges from no information (visitor is *invisible*) when a user has cookies turned off, to knowing which of several possible roles an individual is using during any given session (visitor has *differentiated roles*) (see Table 3.2). Roles a user might have include a home and work role or perhaps multiple work roles.

Table 3.2: The levels of identity.

| Level of Identity | Description |
| --- | --- |
| Invisible | An individual who has not only not registered with the site but has his cookies turned off so that the website can not detect whether he has ever visited before. Lowest level of trust on the site. |
| Anonymous | An individual who has cookies enabled, but has not registered on the site. Shows slightly more trust of the site. |
| Identified | An individual has registered with the site, providing personal information in exchange for the use of personalization features. Shows a high degree of trust on the site. |
| Associated | An individual has both registered with the site and indicated that she/he is associated with a particular team or organization. Shows a very high degree of trust that the site will provide value to him/her and his/her team. |
| Differentiated | An individual who has created multiple profiles on the website for different purposes (e.g., home and business, different business roles). Shows a very high degree of trust on the site. |

### 3.3.8  USER STUDIES

We executed an iterative series of studies, carried out in laboratory and field settings. The studies were a mixture of group sessions (similar to Design Walkthroughs) and individual user evaluation sessions. The user studies were carried out by teams of two with a facilitator who ran the user session and a colleague who recorded the session on videotape and collected verbal comments from participants. Some user sessions were run in the Usability Lab at the Watson Research Center, others were run in field settings in New York City, NY; Raleigh, NC; and Austin, TX. The facilities of the Usability Laboratory enabled observation of the user session in the Studio from the Control Room through use of a one-way mirror and video monitor, as well a range of data collection activities. In the field settings, both the facilitator and the colleague were in a conference room setting with the participant, with a laptop computer for the participant's use and a video camera to record the session.

### 3.3.8.1  Target Users

Participants for the studies were recruited by an external vendor through use of user profiles. Study subjects were drawn from the population of people who are comfortable with the World Wide Web (3+ hours per week usage) and who are at least moderately tech-savvy in their purchasing behavior. They make purchases on the web themselves, but may enlist assistance from other technical experts in the selection of technology to be purchased. Participants received $150 for taking part in a two-hour user session. New groups of target users were recruited for each study.

### 3.3.8.2  User Tasks

The research team created a set of user scenarios that covered purchasing information technology (IT) equipment, maintaining and upgrading the equipment, and getting support for products. The user scenarios featured Pat User (whose gender was randomly assigned in each session) who needed to complete the set of tasks that arose across a period of 18 months in Pat's organization. Thus, we examined both initial visits to a site with personalization features as well as repeated-use scenarios with the same site.

### 3.3.8.3  Procedure

The experimental procedure for both group and individual sessions began with a pre-session questionnaire to collect demographic and job-related information. In the group sessions (Study 1 and 2), the experimenter then read three task scenario scripts to participants accompanied by presentation of a storyboard prototype projected on a large screen. The first scenario concerned buying a server and a mix of desktop and notebook systems for a new department of ten people who were beginning a new project. The second scenario was about upgrading the server to handle the workload of an additional 10 people and buying additional desktop and notebook systems for them. The third scenario focused on buying accessories, in this case zip drives, for Pat's entire department.

Each scenario was presented using a storyboard approach where participants saw screen shots and heard how Pat User used different personalization features to complete specific tasks. Each scenario presented between 5 and 13 personalization features and policies (e.g., presentation of accessories constrained to those compatible with a selected machine previously purchased; presentation of servers compatible with previously determined business characteristics when searching for servers; user control of data). Each scenario presentation was about 20 minutes long and involved the presentation of about 10 creen shots. Following the presentation, the experimenter facilitated a 5-minute discussion with the participants covering the features presented. Comments were recorded on flipcharts in the room. Participants then completed a post-scenario questionnaire and gave their individual ratings for each personalization technique covered on a 7-point scale ranging from "Highly Valuable" to "Not at all Valuable" and design comments in writing. After the third scenario, participants filled out a post-session questionnaire which asked them to identify the most and least valuable features (in relationship to their jobs) from the entire set of three scenarios.

In the individual user sessions (Study 3), six task scenarios about Pat User were provided in written form to the participant, and he or she completed the tasks using interactive personalized prototypes. The order of the presentation of tasks was counterbalanced using a Latin squares design. An example of a task was "purchase additional memory for the laptop computers you bought last month." In individual sessions, participants were encouraged to "think aloud" as they completed tasks. Each scenario included between 3 and 4 features and policies. Participants read the scenario description and then attempted to complete the task described using a prototype system implemented in Microsoft Powerpoint and presented on an IBM Thinkpad.

After each scenario, subjects filled out a questionnaire asking about their reactions to the features presented in the scenario. Following the discussion period with the facilitator, participants filled out a post-scenario questionnaire about the features in the scenario. The participants were asked for written ratings and design comments. At the end of both group and individual sessions, participants completed a post-session questionnaire form and were debriefed before receiving payment. The post-session questionnaire asked the participants to rank order least and most favored features across the scenarios, and they were also asked about expected future interactions with a personalized site.

### 3.3.8.4   User Study 1

For User Study 1, we reviewed the feature list and selected features for inclusion in the following way. First, we wanted to make sure that at least one feature from each of the 14 major categories listed in Table 3.1 was included. Then, we selected a number of features for each scenario as appropriate and illustrated the use of the features in the context of complete tasks. We established a specific number of scenarios for presentation (three in this case) so that we would be able to present the scenario, provide some illustrations of personalization features in use, have a small group discussion, and allow participants to fill out a questionnaire about the features before the next scenario. Three scenarios and the post-session questionnaire fit within the two-hour session time frame.

For Study 1, there were a total of 5 two-hour sessions with 3 to 5 participants in each one, for a total of 20 participants. The study was carried out in a Usability Lab specifically set up for a group session during a week in August, 2001. The participants were all employees of the same company as the researchers, and they volunteered in response to a request to assist in a study which offered a lunch coupon in return for their participation. Participants were recruited based on their answers to screening questions, which indicated that they had input to the decision process for the purchase of a server or workstation in the last year.

### 3.3.8.5   User Study 2

For User Study 2, we reviewed the results of Study 1 and made several small adjustments in the features included (adding 4 features), questionnaires, and scenario and storyboard presentations. Study 2 was conducted over a four day period in October of 2001. There were a total of 5 two-hour group sessions with 2 to 6 participants in each one, for a total of 23 participants. Participants were recruited by an external agency in the New York area. Participants were paid an incentive to participate in the study. The agency used screening questionnaires similar to those used in Study 1. Participants had been involved in the purchase of a server in the last year. About half of them had also been involved in the purchase decision for desktop and notebook systems. The participants were a mix of current ibm.com customers and target customers of the site. Approximately 25% of the participants were recruited from each of the four groups below:

> IT decision makers from traditional companies that purchase UNIX servers, with a company size over 1000 employees

> Business Unit Executives (BUE's) from traditional companies that purchase UNIX servers, with a company size over 1000 employees

> IT decision makers from traditional companies that purchase Intel servers, with a company size of 50-99 employees

> IT decision makers from "next generation" companies that purchase Intel servers, with a company size of 50-99 employees

### 3.3.8.6   User Study 3

Feedback from User Study 1 and 2 was incorporated into the design of User Study 3. This study involved individual participants recruited from the external target customer population who interacted with a hands-on interactive mid-level fidelity prototype to carry out six typical tasks. This is the initial use scenario:

> You are Pat User and you have just become the manager of an IT department that develops and hosts web applications for other companies. You know that you will need to travel in your new job, so you need to purchase a laptop computer. You want to spend less than $2000. As part of your shopping for this laptop, you look at ibm.com. You decide to buy an A Series ThinkPad.

And this is one of the repeated use scenarios:

> Three months have passed since you made your first purchases on the ibm.com site. You are still an IT manager for a small company that provides web-hosting services for other companies. You are now interested in finding a server to provide web-hosting services for a new client. The client wants their data hosted on a separate server for security reasons. You have $8,000 to spend on a server. They need to support 150 clients at a time.

Study 3 was conducted during two weeks in December, 2001. There were a total of 22 two-hour individual user sessions. Participants were recruited by an external agency with expertise in user recruitment. The agency used the same screening questionnaires as those used in Study 2.

Participants had been involved in the purchase of a server in the last year. About half of them had also been involved in the purchase decision for desktop and notebook systems. Participants were paid an incentive to participate in the study.

### 3.3.9   SUMMARY OF APPROACH AND KEY TRADEOFFS

The initial user-centered design activities generated a master list of 75 possible personalization features and a base strategy for personalization, essentially, a set of hypotheses that we explored through a series of three iterative user studies. We leveraged other HCI activities that had been completed or were underway for the Personal Computer Division and Server Group. The outcome of the three studies with target customers was a list of the 12 highest-value features and policies for personalization from a customer point of view, the definition of the personalization strategy for the site, the full documentation of the three iterations of user studies, and the business case for personalization of the site based on customer feedback. This complete set of data enabled the team to develop the Personalization Value Model outlining the value of personalization to customers and the business.

You can always do more with more time; however, one of the critical skills that HCI practitioners must develop and grow is the ability to think on their feet, roll with the punches, and adapt successfully to changing circumstances to successfully complete HCI research that meets or exceeds the sponsor's expectations. This becomes a highly tuned skill over time, to be able to select the right HCI method or tool to use in a particular situation, given time, resources, and context of the research environment. We strongly recommend that new HCI professional hires have the opportunity to team up with more senior HCI experts in order to gain from a transfer of this type of knowledge while involved "hands on" in the research in practice.

## 3.4   HCI RESEARCH RESULTS AND IMPACT

This research was exploratory in nature. The intention was to look at a number of techniques and to accumulate evidence about the value of the techniques in advance of actual development. As such, we relied mainly on participant ratings in a context that simulated real usage as much as possible. We moved from an initial study with internal users who matched the characteristics of the e-commerce target users, to using typical external customers in Studies 2 and 3. We also moved from group walkthroughs in Study 1 and 2 to individual sessions involving completion of task scenarios by participants.

### 3.4.1   ITERATIVE RESEARCH TO IDENTIFY TOP RATED PERSONALIZATION POLICIES AND FEATURES

The group walkthroughs in Study 1 and 2 gave us critical high-level information from users that allowed us to filter the personalization possibilities and identify the high value features. Then, the results of Study 3 provided the researchers with more in-depth design information about the most highly rated personalization features and the impact of these features on site visitation and purchases. We began with a master list of 75 features and 3 policies and identified a final list of 10 features and 2 policies, which together provided a cohesive and valuable personalized user experience on the site that customers stated saved them time and did some of the steps in their jobs for them while ensuring their privacy and control over personal information (see Figure 3.3).

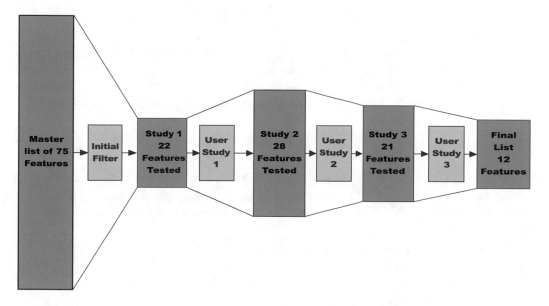

**Figure 3.3:** Iterative HCI research to identify high-value personalization features.

We will summarize the iterative user studies of the personalization policies and features by focusing on the most highly rated features and policies in each study. In general, participants rated all of the features and policies presented above the neutral point on a 7-point scale anchored by "Highly Valuable" and "Not Valuable at all." The average ratings for features over the three studies ranged from 4.4 to 6.4, with 7 being the highest and 1 the lowest possible score. We did not employ a statistical cutoff point for determining when to call a feature highly rated versus not highly rated. We looked for natural and large breaks in the data and used that as a determination point. We planned to follow up with further studies that tested for statistically significant differences in the design alternatives for specific personalization features.

For Study 1, we found that participants wanted to provide only the information necessary, appreciated being able to access histories of past transactions, valued the possibility of contact with human representatives in task context, and would like more efficient search capabilities. Participants reported the highest ratings for the personalization features below (see Table 3.3).

The table provides the wording of the text used on the questionnaires that participants filled out to describe the features and policies. The user study sessions provided richer descriptions of and

**Table 3.3:** The 12 highest rated personalization policies and features. Items in bold text are policies.

1. **You control all the data kept in your profile and can review and edit it at any time.**
2. You can get automatic support updates for the products you own.
3. You can view your purchase order history.
4. You can use the "Help me find what I need" function to help you filter through product choices and make purchase decisions.
5. You can be provided with alternative recommendations for items that are listed on your "Products I Own" page or that are in saved shopping carts and are no longer available.
6. You can view a list of the products you purchased on the site and elsewhere.
7. Once you have logged in, it is clear that the system knows who you are.
8. You can create a wish list that contains items you may be planning to buy in the future if resources allow or there is a special offer.
9. A personal "myXXX" site is created for you when you provide information about yourself.
10. You can save shopping carts with price quotes, availability dates, and contact information in them.
11. You can track the status of your transactions on the xxx .com site.
12. **You are asked to provide only the information needed to allow you to access a feature that helps you complete a particular task.**

context for the features and policies through the demonstrations and immersive user experiences contained in the scenarios and storyboards.

Results from the user ratings for Study 2 and Study 3 are presented in Table 3.4. These were in general agreement with the findings from Study 1. Participants attached greatest value to control over their information and access to past interactions with the company.

Participants thought the "Help Me Find What I Need" feature, which is an instance on context-sensitive help combined with constrained search capabilities, was very valuable (see Figure 3.4).

This innovative feature's value is based on information provided by the user and the system's awareness of the web page that the customer is currently looking at. In the example in Figure 3.4, the system helps users filter the lines of servers down to the ones they are interested in by combining customer information with the web page they are looking at. This user interface design feature was patented by the team in 2003. Users thought the idea of a Personal Book was valuable, with all personal information that they could interact with, and shopping carts with wish list function.

**Table 3.4:** Mean ratings by users and user comment themes from Study 2 and 3 on the 12 highest-rated personalization policies and features. Items in bold text are policies.

| Personalization Features | Mean Rating Study 2 | Mean Rating Study 3 | Comment Themes |
|---|---|---|---|
| **1. User Control of Data** | **6.4** | **6.4** | **Gives me control 77%; Makes it easy 19%; Saves me time 4%.** |
| 2. Automatic Support Alerts | 5.9 | 6.2 | Helps me do my job 53%; Saves me time 27%; Gives me control 12%; Reassures me 4%; I don't like it 4%. |
| 3. Order History | 6.1 | 6.1 | Makes my job easier 100%. |
| 4. Help Me Find What I Need | 5.6 | 6.1 | Makes my job easier 58%; Saves me time 37%; Reassures me 5%. |
| 5. Suggest Product Alt. | 5.6 | 6.0 | Makes my job easier 62%; Saves me time 38%. |
| 6. List of Products You Own | 5.5 | 6.0 | Makes my job easier 53%; Saves me time 37%; Reassures me 10%. |
| 7. Login Feedback | 5.6 | 5.8 | Saves me time 39%; Makes my job easier 46%; Reassures me 15%. |
| 8. Wish List | 5.1 | 5.8 | Makes my job easier 88 %; Design comments 8%; Saves time 4%. |
| 9. Personal Site | 5.4 | 5.6 | Makes my job easier 50%; Saves me time 25%; Gives me control 13%; Didn't notice 12%. |
| 10. Saved Shopping Carts | 5.6 | 5.6 | Makes my job easier 85%; Save me time 15%. |
| 11. Transaction Tracking | 6.2 | 5.6 | Makes my job easier 79%; Saves me time 21%. |
| **12. Only Info Needed** | **6.0** | **5.5** | **Saves me time 73%; Gives me control 27%.** |

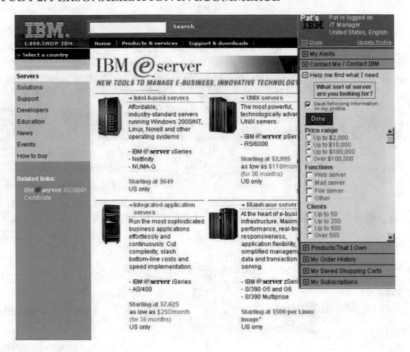

**Figure 3.4:** The "Help Me Find What I Need" feature.

All three personalization policies which were evaluated through the course of the three studies received strong support from target and current customers of the site. Quantitative data was collected on the user control of data and permission marketing policies, and they were in the top ratings by users in each study. The level of identity policy was evaluated in several scenarios through user actions to opt-in to personalization and through comments during and after scenarios. This policy also received strong customer support. Users expressed the desire for access to profiles related to their different roles that they could access through the personal book to make their visits to the site as productive as possible.

Participants were unanimous in stating that they would visit the site more often if personalization features were implemented, and most said that they would make more purchases. While there were differences in the orderings of the features across the three studies, we did not find these to be highly significant. For example, Table 3.4 shows that the second ranked feature in Study 2 (Transaction Tracking) was ranked tied for ninth in Study 3. The feature was still within the highly-rated category for both studies (remember that Table 3.4 does not contain all personalization features tested - only those that were highly rated). We believe that variations in the individual and group tasks contributed to these minor differences.

## 3.4.2    BUSINESS CASE SUPPORT

All three studies included post-session questions which measured participants' attitudes concerning the likelihood of increased visits and purchases by them from a site which was personalized by adding the features they identified as valuable. While we realize that such measures might not accurately reflect actual future behavior, we believed they would offer valuable input to our customer organization in making decisions about development funding. When asked the question "If the features you indicated as of highest value to you were implemented on the XXX site, would you be more likely to use the site?," all 23 users in Study 2 and all 22 users in Study 3 responded "Yes." The modal (most frequent) response to the follow-up question of how often they thought they would visit the site was "10+" more times during the course of a year for both Study 2 and Study 3.

When asked if the participants thought they would be more likely to purchase from the site if the features of highest value were implemented and appropriate products were available and within their budgets, 22 out of 23 participants in Study 2 and all 22 participants in Study 3 responded "Yes." One Study 2 participant responded "Maybe." The participants' modal and mean responses in terms of the number of additional purchases they would make in a year were the range of 3-4 purchases. The modal response on the amount of the purchase was in the $5,001-$10,000 range. The mean response for participants was 5.8 in Study 2 and 5.7 in Study 3, with a rating of "5" representing a purchase of $2,501-$5,000 and a rating of "6" representing a purchase of $5,001- $10,000.

We employed the target user data from these questions to build a business case for the financial value of adding personalization features to the web site. Major assumptions for the business case were that projections were based on the following:

1. Call center and web based revenue for the Americas,

2. The personal computer and server areas of the site only,

3. The target population of customers covered in the user studies, and

4. A time period of one year.

Projections of increased site traffic and increased purchase transactions were added to existing mathematical and financial models relating site visits to revenue, and a significant business case for the value of personalization to the e-commerce site resulted. The costs of implementation of the top-ranked personalization features were included in the business case as well. This projection was based on user statements about what they thought they would do rather than on measures of actual performance. However, since the participants were asked these questions after immersive personalized experiences where they completed tasks relevant to their critical day-to-day tasks, such projections were viewed as better founded than most business case estimates in software development.

## 3.4.3    THE PERSONALIZATION VALUE MODEL

Based on the affinity diagrams from the contextual inquiry data analyses of the business requirements collected from the ibm.com stakeholders in the initial research for this project and the comments made by external customers and target customers during the immersive personalization experience in Study 3, we developed a Personalization Value Model (see Figure 3.5). The model begins with a customer's first time opt-in to personalization. The system asks the customer for permission to use the minimal amount of personal information necessary to more efficiently and effectively complete the task the customer is currently on the site to complete. The customer agrees and provides the

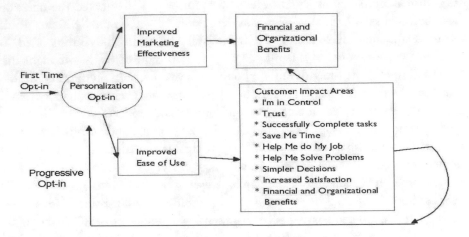

**Figure 3.5:** The personalization value model.

information, and in exchange, the customer receives immediate value in the high quality completion of his task. The customer experiences improved ease of use in accomplishing tasks on the site through personalization, and they place very high value in being in control of their personal data.

In illustrating the Personalization Value Model, one customer, echoing many, told us "It makes me feel comfortable to be in control of my information. It makes me feel I can trust a company that is not looking to control or sell my information." Customers stated that they would value the ability to complete tasks successfully and quickly on the site with personalization, and that the personalization functionality would simplify their jobs in small ways. As one customer expressed it: "If you can save me time or do some of the steps in my job for me so that I don't have to do them, that's real value to me, and you've got my business."

Customers also thought that the personalization functionality such as the "Products I Own" and the "Help Me Find What I Need" tabs in the Personal Book allowed them to solve their own problems and made their decision-making simpler. Customers expressed increased satisfaction with their personalized user experience on the site and stated that it would have financial and organizational benefits for them as well. The customer experience with personalization provides a feedback loop to a progressive opt-in to personalization; they receive more value as more personal information is disclosed. The top loop of the model shows the business value of personalization to ibm.com. With customer permission, personalization would enable ibm.com to serve customers more effectively and efficiently as they inquire about information and make purchases or come to the site for after-sales support. Personalization would allow ibm.com to improve marketing effectiveness as customers self-select to receive promotional or other marketing information on specific products. These combined benefits produce financial and organizational benefits for ibm.com.

### 3.4.4   PERSONALIZATION STRATEGY AND RECOMMENDATIONS

Based on analysis of both the quantitative and qualitative data collected, the research team recommended to ibm.com that the organization implement personalization on the site with the three personalization policies including user control of data, permission marketing, and levels of identity at the core of the approach. There were nine specific personalization features which together with the three policies made a set of twelve concepts to implement to provide a highly satisfying personalized user experience to visitors at the site. The two personalization features about wish lists and saved shopping carts were combined into one function as customers saw it as one. Similarly, four personalization features which together formed a cohesive inventory-based personalization function through the "Products I Own" tab in the Personal Book were grouped together as one comprehensive feature. The set of twelve is listed in Table 3.5 below. They are listed in their relative order of importance as suggested by the customer data.

As can be seen in the table, user control of data was the top valued personalization function. Customers saw this policy as the essential basis for their willingness to opt-in to a personalized user experience on the site. Customers were excited about the flexibility of being able to access and use their data through the Personal Book from any page on the site. Customers thought that automatic support updates on their products, delivered either to their Personal Book or to their email address or as a phone message as preferred, would provide great value and save them a lot of time and trouble by having proactive alerts and updates sent to them, completing steps for them that they normally do themselves at this time. The "Products That I Own" inventory-based personalization function was viewed as providing ongoing superb value to customers. This function would allow them to quickly and correctly find compatible accessories for products they own, would simply decision making by enabling customers to get recommendations on purchasing alternatives that would be compatible with previous purchases (e.g., buying additional laptops or office systems for an organization over time), and being able to track delivery of orders and review their information technology purchases by group, department, or organization. Customers saw great value in being able to share this information within their organizations and thought that this functionality would handle responsibilities for them that they were allocating other resources, time and energy to at this time.

The context-aware "Help Me Find What I Need" function provides customers a way of quickly and effectively constraining options based on their needs when searching for information. Permission marketing is valued as a means of earning customers' sense of trust and reliability in working with the site and in developing business relationships they can count on. The Login Feedback, Universal Profile, and Levels of Identity together provide valuable information to customers that the site knows who they are, regardless of where they are on the site, and that the information in their

**Table 3.5:** Recommendations for top twelve ranked personalization policies and features, based on empirical research with target users.

| Personalization Description | Policy or Feature |
| --- | --- |
| User Control of Data: You control all the data in your profile and can review and edit it at any time. | Policy |
| Automatic Support: You can get automatic updates for the products that you own. | Feature |
| Products That I Own: You can view 'Products That I Own" and get alternative recommendations for items that are no longer available, find compatible accessories and upgrades, and track/review current and past transactions. | Feature |
| Help Me Find What I Need: You can use "Help Me Find What I Need" to help you filter through product choices and make purchase decisions. | Feature |
| Permission Marketing: You are asked to provide only the information needed to allow you to access the feature that helps you complete a task. | Policy |
| Login Feedback: Once you have logged in, it is clear that the system knows who you are. | Feature |
| Universal Profile: The information you provide is active across the entire site. | Feature |
| Future Purchase Considerations: You can save shopping carts and indicate that you want to hear about special promotions on items in that cart. | Feature |
| Personal Book: A personal "my IBM" site is created for you when you provide information about yourself. | Feature |
| Levels of Identity: You can adopt the appropriate level of identity for the particular task on the site. | Policy |
| Adaptive Presentation: The pages displayed are adapted based on your recent navigation path (implicit data with session life span). | Feature |
| Contact IBM in Context: You can communicate with IBM in the context of your profile and your current task. | Feature |

profiles associated with their chosen levels of identity for their current tasks can be used with their permission to provide better and more timely service to them.

Customers were excited about the idea of saving shopping carts and being able to indicate they wanted to hear about special promotions on the items in the cart. They wanted to be able to designate the period of time for the shopping cart to be saved and to be able to share the shopping cart information with others in their organization. Customers thought that the use of implicit navigation data to adapt the presentation of information could be valuable if use of the data with permission was limited to a session life span. Customers liked this idea in concept but thought that the technology had not matured sufficiently to guarantee its usefulness.

And last, but not least, customers valued the ability to contact IBM in the context of their current task. They thought that being able to ask a specific question in a "chat-like" session while sharing the page they were viewing with IBM would enable that to get a quick and accurate answer to questions. For more involved questions, customers said they would prefer to speak on the phone with an IBM representative whom they have had previous interactions with and with whom they would be comfortable sharing their profile data.

The research team suggested to ibm.com that the organization extend the research in other key area of the site such as software, support, and services to confirm where the results generalize and where changes were needed. Research was conducted at the same time by another research team in the support area which validated the research reported in this case study. We also recommended that ibm.com develop guidelines to inform development work in this space and the team participated in the creation of these standards. The ibm.com organization worked to develop and implement the infrastructure to accommodate the personalization features recommended above. Planning then proceeded on studies to define the roll out of selected functions across the 4 million pages and 2,200 sub sites of the organization.

### 3.4.5    CONCLUSIONS

This research was conducted to achieve three goals: (1) identify potential personalization features, (2) explore these features with potential users to understand their value, and (3) prioritize the list of features with respect to cost and benefit information to customers and providers. The scope of this research effort included commerce and support use cases for servers, desktops, notebooks, and related accessories. We believe the results are valid for the targeted customers and their core use case scenarios.

We researched the personalization requirements for a portion of the e-commerce site. We believe the research needed to be extended to determine what features are best for other parts of the site as the products and services in other parts of the site represent additional parts of the personalization value model (i.e., other commerce types and other user characteristics).

Our research in developing a personalization strategy for an e-commerce organization led us to develop a framework on what it means to personalize (or tailor) an interactive experience. Our focus was on identifying the overall value of personalization with an emphasis on the e-commerce environment. Our research indicated that personalization should not be thought of as a single feature, but rather should be considered as a space in which different features can have different values depending on the user and business contexts.

Further research is needed to explore this Personalization Feature Space (PFS) through a systematic examination of personalization policies (e.g., permission marketing, user control of data), feature categories (e.g., collaborative filtering, click stream analysis), user characteristics (e.g., predisposition to trust, interaction goal), and business context (e.g., product offering, business goals). We believe that the effectiveness of personalization efforts are a function of four components (i.e., Effectiveness = f (policy, feature, user context, business context)). The identification of the exact functional relationships is a rich area for future research.

## 3.5    LESSONS LEARNED FROM THE HCI RESEARCH

We learned a variety of lessons about the HCI approach taken in this empirical research. These lessons helped the team to make the most of the time, resources and existing knowledge of the research domain. Each of these lessons will be discussed below. The lessons dealt with both the HCI tools and methods used in the iterative research on personalization in ecommerce as well as the lessons drawn related to the content of the research findings themselves as demonstrated in the data collected using the various HCI engineering methods during the course of the study.

First, the team was gratified to learn of the value and efficiency of the brainstorming sessions on the research topic with experts in the organization worldwide. The asynchronous virtual brainstorming sessions raised a wide range of ideas and issues and increased the team's understanding of the research underway in different labs around the world. Based on our sponsor's objectives and timetable, we were able to filter the information and incorporate many ideas into the research on the base set of personalization features. Seems valuable for HCI experts in different organizations and circumstances to consider methods for tailoring this brainstorming approach to their needs in seeking the knowledge of experts in a particular domain.

Next, competitive evaluations have been employed for many years in the HCI domain as a means of understanding the current state of the field in a particular topic area. The competitive evaluations of personalization aspects of the user experience at related sites provided valuable information that assisted the team in setting the objectives for the current organization.

In many circumstances today, HCI practitioners and researchers are under very tight time constraints in completing their work. However, the tried and true value of literature reviews was again shown in the research in the domain of personalization and ecommerce. The team was able to avoid certain pitfalls as well as include some ideas based on published research in the area. It does take time to read the literature. In many of the papers reviewed for conferences and journals over the last 5-10 years, it is troubling to see the authors' lack of understanding, either in depth or breadth, of particular topics. People very rarely cite research from more than five years in the past or demonstrate knowledge of it in framing a problem or discussing options related to a topic. Yet, as history teaches all of us, those who fail to understand the past, are doomed to repeat it.

The team's interviews with the sponsors enabled the identification of their business require-ments. Having a clear statement of these requirements enabled the team to determine how to use the available time and resources to the best advantage.

Conducting HCI work with iterations of prototypes to hone the design of a solution is extremely valuable. Over many years of research, the team has found that being able to iterate two to three times on a design with feedback from target customers is critical in reaching an optimal design solution. Often, breakthroughs are made in the third iteration that did not appear possible earlier on. In this case, study, design updates were made to the flow, feature functionality, and language and graphics across the three iterations. It's of great value to HCI research to allow for multiple design iterations and feedback sessions with the target users. The results can be discussed with architects in the area and innovative solutions may occur over time.

These iterations in prototyping and design need to be balanced with the difficulty in recruiting participants. particularly if the target users are difficult to recruit due to time and resource constraints. The team's use of internal participants in Study 1 who matched the target user profile provided an extremely effective way to shake out and get early feedback on the study materials, the early version of the prototype, and the overall usability session. Study 1 enabled the team to identify issues, both large and small, with format and content of the usability sessions so that when these sessions were run with the recruited external customers and target customers, those sessions were more productive and valuable to the research team.

The team was impressed with the wealth of qualitative user data collected during the study. Even with the eight months, we had for the series of studies, we did not have the opportunity to mine the data for all the nuggets there. There were two lessons here: 1) be aware of the volume of data you will have to analyze and 2) build in time in the schedule to conduct these analyses.

Turning now to the methods used and results obtained in Study 2 and 3 with the target users, it was interesting to note the general consistency in the findings between Study 2 and Study 3, given the differences in the methods used in the two studies. In Study 2, participants were in a group design walkthrough and did not directly interact with the system; they reacted to a presentation by the experimenter. Though this presentation was designed to be engaging, it still represented a passive experience. For Study 3, participants were provided tasks to complete similar those used in the previous studies, but they interacted with a prototype personalized system to complete them. The similarity in the results across the two studies provided an indication of concurrent validity in the use of the different methods. It's important in the HCI domain, to determine where and when different tools can be used to obtain critical data for design and development.

On the one hand, the cross-validation over user studies strengthens our confidence in the general findings. On another level, it provides some evidence about the value of the group technique. Such group studies are often easier to conduct at early design stages, but uncertainty about the validity of the results can cause researchers to limit the use of such techniques. The research team's experience and results with the mixture of group and individual walkthrough and user study HCI methods validated our team's use of these methods in previous research and encouraged us to use this mixture of techniques in later research in other domains, where the use of the methods was again very successful (Karat et al. (2001, 2002); Karat, J. (2003); Brodie et al. (2004); Karat et al. (2005, 2006); and Karat and Karat (2008)).

For more information about the series of research studies completed on personalization in ecommerce, please see several different chapters by our team in the book *Designing Personalized User Experiences in eCommerce* (Karat et al., 2004). This book is an edited volume of chapters by a group of international experts covering a variety of personalization topics in eCommerce.

CHAPTER 4

# Case Study 3: Security and Privacy Policy Management Technologies

## 4.1 INTRODUCTION

This case study describes a line of privacy, privacy and security, and policy research that took place from 2003 until 2009. Due to the breadth of work involved, the case study will cover the significant points across these years of research. For further information on the details of the research, please see the following publications:

- Karat et al. (2003), for a discussion of privacy requirements for the emerging privacy policy technology;

- Brodie et al. (2004), a paper on early user and system requirements for privacy policy technology;

- Karat et al. (2005c), an IJHCS journal article that provides an overview of the first three years of research;

- Karat et al. (2005), for a book chapter on the design of usable security technology, and an overview of HCI methods for different phases of the usability lifecycle;

- Brodie et al. (2005), a SOUPS conference paper on the policy prototype technology and functionality;

- Karat et al. (2006), a CHI 2006 conference paper on the SPARCLE policy authoring tool with detailed analysis of user errors and preferences;

- Brodie et al. (2006), a SOUPS conference paper on the natural language processing technology and related data;

- Karat et al. (2007), a CACM article on the need for usable security and privacy technology in personal information management;

- Karat et al. (2007b), a book chapter on privacy and security policy aspects of personal information management, an expanded treatment of the CACM article above;

- Reeder et al. (2007), an INTERACT conference paper on further detailed empirical study of SPARCLE authoring;

- Karat and Karat (2008), a SSCR journal article on the privacy and security policy aspects of pervasive computing;

- Ni et al. (2008), an ACM TCL journal article on privacy policy architecture completed as part of the OCR project;

- Karat et al. (2008), an HCI handbook chapter on privacy, security and trust;

- Brodie et al. (2008), an IEEE Policy conference paper on the ITA policy authoring and analysis prototype;

- Karat et al. (2009), an IBM JRD journal article on security and privacy policy architecture completed as part of the OCR project;

- Bertino et al. (2009), an IBM JRD journal article on policy analysis completed as part of the OCR project; and

- Calo et al. (2010), a book chapter covering two years of fundamental research on policy authoring and management in coalition networks as part of the ITA project.

## 4.2    BACKGROUND ON THE DOMAIN OF STUDY

The rapid advancement of the use of information technology in industry, government, and academia makes it much easier to collect, transfer, and store sensitive information of a variety of types around the world. Questions have arisen internationally, in public and private sectors and the media, about the use and protection of personal information (PI) (Kobsa, A., 2002). Society is faced with technical challenges that result from inadequate consideration of security and privacy issues in architecting information systems. Making systems secure and enabling appropriate attention to privacy issues requires more than just a technology focus. Usability has been identified as a major challenge to moving the results of security and privacy research into use in real systems (CRA, 2003).

Our team views privacy, which depends on strong security, as a complex social issue concerned with individuals' rights to know what information is collected about them and how it might be used (Karat et al., 2005,c). Questions regarding who has what rights to information about us for what purposes become more important as we move toward a world in which it is technically possible to know just about anything about just about anyone (Karat et al., 2005b). As stated by Adams and Sasse (2001): 'Most invasions of privacy are not intentional but due to designers' inability to anticipate how this data could be used, by whom, and how this might affect users.'

In 2003, our team began a line of research with the goal of creating usable privacy policy technologies for individuals and organizations. As the research evolved, the goals and scope expanded to privacy and security access control. The first product based on our research was released in 2007 and is called IBM Secure Perspective (IBM Secure Perspective, 2007). For business reasons, our team was later asked to raise the research goal and focus to the creation of usable policy technologies for authoring and management of policies in a wide range of domains including operational business processes, network security, and physical security in buildings, in addition to the privacy and security policy areas we began the research focus on.

In the most recent years of our team's research, the research goal has been extended to include the creation of usable policy technologies that can be employed by dynamic coalition groups in mobile ad hoc networks (MANETs) in rugged and hostile locations. A further goal is to investigate the use of these policy technologies to help with environmental challenges through more efficient and informed use of water and power by individuals, organizations, and communities of various sizes.

In this chapter, we will follow the case study of the research chronologically over five years as the focus progressed from privacy policy, to privacy and security policy, to policy in a wide variety of domains and situations. We will provide an overview of the research from concept to product release, and ongoing post-release research. The discussion will cover the research approach and methods, results (only in terms of how the results led to the follow-on decisions and actions), and what was learned in the different phases. Let's begin with an introduction to privacy.

Privacy of information held in information systems depends on security – the ability to protect system resources from harmful attack or unauthorized access. Security is an essential component in systems that house personal information on employees, clients, constituents, students, customers, and patients. As context for this area of HCI research, it is critical to understand unique challenges to HCI research related to privacy and security as compared to other domains.

First and foremost, the use of security and privacy solutions is generally not the user's main goal. Users value and want security and privacy functionality, but they regard this functionality as secondary to completing their primary tasks (e.g., completing a transaction or communicating with others). Second, a wide range of users must be able to successfully use the solutions as compared to the past when security solutions in particular were designed with a highly trained and dedicated technical user in mind. Third, the risk of the negative impact of usability problems is higher for security and privacy applications than for many other types of systems. Finally, users must be able to easily update security and privacy solutions to accommodate frequent changes in legislation, regulation, and organizational requirements.

HCI practitioners need to consider the unique points above as they work to understand the users for a privacy or security solution, and their skills, strengths, and vulnerabilities; the users' activities and goals, and the context of use in which these actions takes place. And to create usable privacy and security solutions, HCI experts must consider how the mechanisms that they are designing for a solution may be abused. As with all HCI activities, it is critical that the professionals be ready to cost-justify the proposed solution.

While there is considerable consensus around a set of high level principles regarding the protection of privacy in information technology (OECD Guidelines, 1980), very little has been done to implement privacy policies through technology. Privacy policy enforcement remains largely a human process, and the policies that organizations present to customers are generally very vague (e.g., "Customer service reps will only use your personal information for the efficient conduct of our business"). There are emerging standards for the content and display of privacy policies on websites (Cranor, L., 2002), but these are standardized XML schemas of the policy content that do not specify how the policy is implemented by the organization, and there is no ability to check on the compliance of a website with its privacy policy posted on the website. The reality is that there is limited capability to have technology implement access and use limitations that people might expect from a policy statement like "We will not share your information with a third party without your consent." A user's ability to select to 'opt out' regarding certain organizational actions is often the extent of user control over privacy policies in interacting with organizations. While much privacy related research and development is focused on the end user's control of information on websites and pervasive devices, this case study focuses on privacy research conducted at the organizational level necessary for privacy policy authoring, implementation and auditing (see Karat et al. (2005,c)).

Parties involved in information exchanges have implicit or explicit privacy policies with regard to the use of information. These privacy policies are held both to the person whom the information is about and by the organization collecting and using the information. While there has been some research on the generally implicit policies of end users whose PI is being collected and used (often called data-subjects), the majority of the research is on the policies of the organizations collecting the information. Smith, J. (1993) described such organizational policies and also noted the lack of technology to enforce the policies. He described the unstructured ways in which organizations create privacy policies. These methods have changed only slightly in the 15 years since his research was published, even in light of the plethora of privacy legislation in the past few years and attention given to privacy breaches by the media. Much research and implementation remains to be done to address the needs in the privacy policy space. In our research, we focused on both the individual data subject and the organizational privacy policy needs by addressing the gap between policy and practice.

## 4.2.1    PRIVACY POLICY STRUCTURE

The International Association of Privacy Professionals (IAPP) reports research results showing that 98% of companies have privacy policies. Generally, organizations have proprietary, internal policies that state more detailed rules about information handling within an organization and then external policies which describe the policy in higher-level, abstract terms intended to inform the data subjects about use of their information. We focused in our research on internal policies, largely because they describe actual data handling procedures in organizations. These policies have a fairly specific format that describes who can use what information for what purposes (Ponemon Institute and IAPP, 2004). Organizations generally have a number of internal privacy policies, some to address use of data about internal employees, and others to address use of data about individuals with which the organization interacts (e.g., customers, patients, clients). Privacy policies include a number of rules governing the use of data-subject's information. Privacy policy rules include the following elements:

user,

data element,

purpose,

action or use,

condition, and

obligations (OASIS Standard, 2005; Ashley et al., 2003).

The first four of these elements can be said to be required of any good policy rule, and the last two are optional (see Figure 4.1).

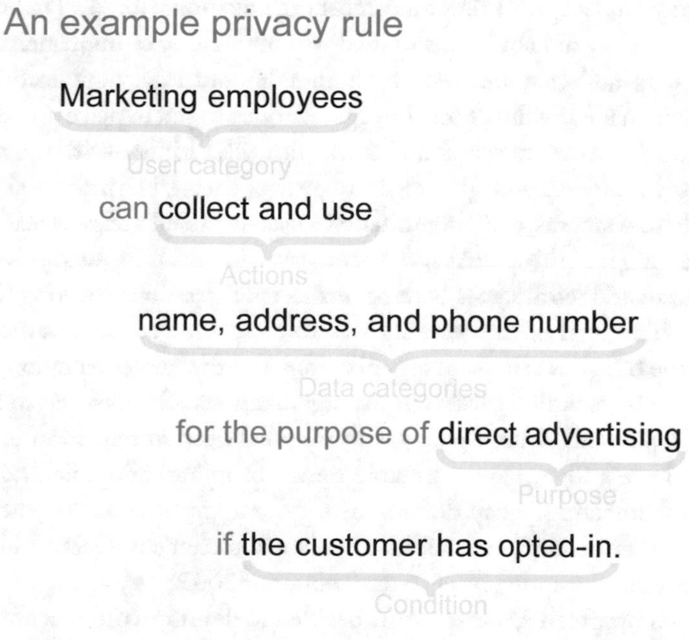

An example privacy rule

Marketing employees

User category

can collect and use

Actions

name, address, and phone number

Data categories

for the purpose of direct advertising

Purpose

if the customer has opted-in.

Condition

**Figure 4.1:** Elements in a privacy policy rule.

The data user who accesses the data may be acting in a particular role in regard to a purpose. For example, doctors may read protected health information for medical treatment and diagnosis. In many privacy policies and legislation, granting or denying access occurs conditionally and incurs an obligation on the data user to take additional actions. For example, a medical researcher may read protected health information for medical research if the patient has previously explicitly authorized release (i.e., the condition) and the patient is notified within 90 days of the release of information (i.e., the obligation).

In our research, we learned that target users of the policy technology did not differentiate between condition and obligation elements, rather, they viewed them all as 'conditions,' so we label both types of these elements as 'conditions' in the policy technology interfaces. The elements are handled quite differently under the covers, but they are presented in the simplest and most understandable way to the user.

## 4.3    PURPOSES OF THE HCI RESEARCH

In 2003, in discussions with representatives from one of the product divisions, our team learned that a new customer need was emerging regarding privacy technology capabilities. Customers were considering the impact of new legislation as well as changing cultural norms and wanted to get out ahead of the changing landscape. At that time, most organizations stored PI in heterogeneous server system environments. They did not have a unified way of defining or implementing privacy policies that encompassed data collected and used by both Web and legacy applications across different server platforms. This made it difficult for the organizations to put in place proper management and control of PI, for the data users to access and work with the PI inline with the privacy policies and for the data subjects to understand rights regarding use of their PI (Anton et al., 2004).

To address these concerns, our team initiated a user-centered design research program in 2003 with the goal of creating a highly usable and customer-validated, integrated privacy policy management capability that would work across heterogeneous configurations covering all PI data to reduce organizational risk. The goal of the research was to close the gap of execution between written policies created by the business experts in organizations and the implementation of those policies on organizations systems by technical experts in the organizations. The idea was to have the policy tool enable systems to implement written policy with minimal need to transform it. The goal included enabling people to have a logical and verifiable thread from authoring, analyzing, and visualizing privacy policies, to connecting policy definition to system entities (implementation), to checking policy compliance though compliance audits of policy enforcement decision logs. These activities were completed between the spring of 2003 and winter of 2005.

As the research progressed, our sponsors decided to develop a product around the core policy capability we had created and release it externally. The first release of IBM Secure Perspective was available in May of 2007 (IBM Secure Perspective, 2007). Our team had transferred our research prototype to our sponsors at the end of 2005, and our HCI research focus in 2006 continued to involve investigating and creating capabilities for the end to end policy management solution while also working with the development team in productizing the tool. Business focus stipulated that we lead with security policy management capability in the first release of the product, with privacy and other policy domains to follow.

After release of the product IBM Secure Perspective in early 2007, the team focused internally on extending the end-to-end policy management capability by creating a policy grammar development environment that would enable customers to adapt Secure Perspective to handle policies written for a wide range of domains including security and privacy access control policies to electronic data, to network security policies, operational business process policies, and physical security policies for buildings. The team raised the research focus from security and privacy policies to policy management in general. We defined the test case for the policy grammar development environment to be the successful creation of new network security policy grammars for the network security domain.

An Open Collaborative Research (OCR) project was begun on privacy and security policy frameworks and included research partners Lorrie Cranor and her team at Carnegie Mellon University and Elisa Bertino and her team at Purdue University. The goals of the research project were to do great policy technology research and publish it, seed the growth of an international set of professionals focused on policy technology, and provide some open source technology for the international community.

Following the OCR project, the US Army Research Laboratory and the UK Ministry of Defense sponsored a consortium of academic, industry and government partners to conduct fundamental research on mobile ad hoc networks used by dynamic coalitions around the world. Our team was asked to create a simplified method of policy authoring for coalition operations. The team researched a variation of the structured list approach of policy authoring that we called template-based authoring. The goal was to be able to author policies to control access to a variety of sensors and other peripheral devices, and have the data collected by the devices, on a wireless network. The team has worked the last couple of years to create and refine the template version of the authoring tool, and now we are focused on enriching the tool with a usable template authoring environment to enable adaptation of the tool to new policy domains. We are expanding the focus of this second approach to policy management from security and network access control required by the coalitions to civilian applications in a wide range of domains including operational business process policies, privacy policies for social networking, and through environmental policy technology to aid the more efficient and informed use of water and power by individuals, groups, and communities of all sizes.

## 4.4    RESEARCH APPROACH AND TRADEOFFS

In 2003, our team initiated a user-centered design research program on organizational privacy capabilities. We employed a variety of usability methods to progress from identifying organizational privacy concerns and needs to designing and evaluating prototypes and design trade-offs. This work included (1) identifying privacy needs within organizations through email survey questionnaires, (2) refining the needs through in-depth interviews with privacy-responsible individuals in organizations, (3) designing and validating a prototype of a technology approach to meeting organizational privacy needs through onsite scenario-based walkthroughs with target users, and (4) collecting empirical data in a controlled Usability Laboratory test to understand the usability of privacy policy authoring methods included in our proposed design.

We then collaborated with the product group on continued research with target users in the creation of the product based on the research prototype. As time went on, we collaborated with groups in academia, industry and government on publicly available research and with additional groups within our organization to innovate, improve and generalize the policy technology capabilities.

### 4.4.1   IDENTIFYING AND REFINING ORGANIZATIONAL PRIVACY NEEDS

We completed the initial interview research to identify organizational privacy needs and increase our in-depth understanding of them through two research steps. The first step was an email survey of 51 participants to identify key privacy concerns and technology needs. We used an email survey as it was important to get representation from around the world and onsite travel for this purpose was viewed as impractical. We recruited early adopters and visionary participants in privacy from industry and government organizations in North America, Europe and Asia.

Participants were recruited through a variety of social-networking mechanisms as was little in the way of established professional organizations in the domain to work with at this time in 2003. In privacy breakout sessions at professional conferences, we made brief announcements about our research and asked if participants would be interested and willing to have us contact them about it in the future. We followed up with people who had given us permission to contact them for this purpose. As we began to meet and establish trusted relationships with these innovators and early adopters in privacy, we asked them to give us referrals to their peers in other organizations. We contacted them with a brief explanatory email and if they agreed to work with us, included them as well. In this manner, we were able to gain the valuable perspective of the emerging international professional privacy community.

As these individuals were volunteering to work with us, we decided to make the email survey brief and to the point. The survey had three questions and took about 10 minutes to complete.

There were three questions:

1. What are your top privacy concerns regarding your organization?

2. What types of privacy functionality would you like to have available to address your privacy concerns regarding your organization?

3. At this time, what action is your organization taking to address the top privacy concerns you listed above?

Based on previous interactions with privacy innovators, there were a set of choices provided that people could select one or more of as well as the option to define the answers in their own words. Participants were encouraged to provide some comments to describe the rationale for their choices as well.

The group of 51 privacy survey respondents included 23 individuals from industry and 28 in-dividuals from government. We had identified a group of 64 potential participants, and the response rate to the email questionnaire was approximately 80%. This response rate was very high (for most social science research, a response rate of 15% to surveys is the norm) and indicated a high level of engagement of these individuals with the topic of privacy. All participants in this and all other phases of the research were promised that their data would be kept confidential and that data would be presented only in a summarized or de-identified format.

As a way of thanking participants for your input, we promised to provide them with a de-identified summary of the results. The participants told us that given that this was leading edge research that they were very interested in, that being given access to the report was quite valuable to them. Because of the very positive reaction to us sending out summaries of the research to the participants, we decided to provide these research reports to each set of participants at each stage in the project.

As a second step in understanding the user and system requirements, we conducted individual in-depth interviews with a sub-set of 13 participants who completed the email survey. The 13 participants were selected to provide geographic representation as well as representation in the government and industry domains. The results of the email survey guided the structure and content of the interview questions. The goals of the in-depth interviews were to build a deeper understanding of the participants' and their organizations' views regarding privacy, their privacy concerns, and the value they perceived in the desired privacy technology they spoke of in the context of scenarios of use involving PI in their organizations. The majority of each interview session was centered on discussion of a scenario of use provided by the respondent regarding PI information flow in their organization and follow-up questions related to it. We wanted to identify and understand examples of how PI flowed through business processes in the organization, the strengths and weaknesses of these processes involving PI, the manual and automated processes to address privacy, and the additional privacy functionality they need in the context of these scenarios.

The participants were representatives of government and industry in Europe, Canada, and the US. All of the interviews were completed by telephone in about an hour. The interviews consisted of seven open-ended questions and some follow-up questions.

We made the tradeoff of conducting the interviews over the phone rather than in person due to practical constraints. Given that an initial relationship with the participants had been established through the first email survey and the distribution of the reports back to the participants, the phone interview format worked remarkably well. All parties on the call were very interested in privacy issues and privacy technology, and thus generally within the first ten minutes the interview became quite comfortable for everyone concerned. During the interviews, one researcher led the interview while another took notes. Notes were transcribed within 24 hours and the team of researchers would discuss the notes until consensus was reached on content. The goal at this stage was to define user and system requirements, and to create a set of core task scenarios regarding privacy that would guide the rest of the project.

The results of the email and interview research guided the development of the privacy management prototype in the third phase of the research. We called our prototype of a privacy policy management tool SPARCLE for Server Privacy ARchitecture and CapabiLity Enablement. These were the goals of this third phase:

- Determine if the privacy functionality that had been identified for inclusion in SPARCLE from the first two phases of the research actually met the users' needs,

- Identify any new requirements,

- Determine the effectiveness of the interaction methods for the targeted user community, and

- Gain contextual information to inform the lower level design of the tool.

We started by validating the core task scenarios we had created in the previous phase by attending breakout sessions on privacy at additional conferences and presenting the scenarios to the people there. We gained valuable feedback and made some slight additions to the scenarios. Then we started with design sketches and iterated through low to mid-fidelity prototypes, which we evaluated first with internal stakeholders and then with target customers who were concerned about privacy. The design iterations on the prototype were guided by core user scenarios about two fictional privacy and compliance officers in an organization, Pat User and Terry Specialist, and how they used the prototype to author and implement privacy policies, and audit the privacy logs for compliance.

One of the key design decisions we made concerned the methods for authoring policies. The research had shown in many organizations, privacy policies are created by committees that included business process specialists, lawyers, and security and information technologists. Based on the range of skills represented, we hypothesized that different methods of authoring within the tool would be valuable to users. We designed SPARCLE to support users with a variety of skills by allowing individuals responsible for privacy policy creation to define these policies using either natural language (NL) with a guide that described privacy policy rule formats or a structured, drop-down list format that gave users a template for policy rule creation. In the natural language method, we employed the use of natural language processing technologies to identify policy elements, and after review by the user for accuracy, transformed the policy rules into machine usable code. The structured format method was automatically transformed into machine usable code. We designed SPARCLE to keep the two authoring methods synchronized at all times so that users in their different work flows, could move back and forth between them as desired for viewing and editing purposes during different activities in policy management.

The use of natural language processing technologies in the tool was a research approach our team decided to investigate. We hypothesized that this was possible, and that users would find it valuable. It was very exciting research that led us to collaborate with several different areas within the Research Division in order to have the required expertise on the team. Many teams would not have been able to follow this course. As always, research approaches need to be determined within the time, resource, and skills available to the team. This was an exceptional opportunity. The research had considerable risk and it worked. The team filed many patents and the possibility of using natural language for policy authoring and communication at the business level of an organization was seen by customers as very attractive and valuable, while the tie through the policy transformation into machine usable code enabled customers to close the gap between the business side of an organization and the technical side that implements the operational solutions for business processes.

During this third phase of the project, in parallel with the iterative design work occurring, we conducted a series of field usability walkthrough evaluations of the tool with representatives from the three domain areas of banking/finance, health care, and government. These three domain areas had surfaced during our research as the top areas for privacy technology. Recruiting participants from Europe, Canada, and the US for these usability walkthrough sessions held onsite at a customer organization was a significant effort. The target group of emerging privacy professionals was very specialized and they had limited time available. We identified these individuals through calls for participation at privacy sessions at industry conferences, by contacting and getting referrals from participants in earlier studies, and by employing professional and personal contacts within our department.

These research feedback sessions were scheduled as 90-minute privacy walkthrough sessions onsite at the participant's work locations. Scenario-based scripts were created and used to control for the presentation of information. The sessions began with brief introductions of the researchers and the participants. Then the scenario-based walkthrough of the prototype began. One researcher would facilitate the session by leading the group through the scenario while the second researcher would demonstrate the prototype's capabilities, and the computer screen was displayed on a wall for the small group to see. There were several modules or sections within the scenario script. At the end of each one, we would have a group discussion and then participants would each complete questionnaire on the capabilities illustrated by the prototype. This research approach was taken to maximize the feedback received from the participants. The group discussions raised a number of different issues, and then the individual data sheets allowed the participants to rank order issues and also define further issues. At the end of these sessions, participants were invited to have hands on interaction with the tool.

A wealth of data was collected from these sessions. The primary purpose of the sessions was to gather qualitative data to help the team better understand the needs of organizational users for privacy functionality and also understand areas of the prototype that needed to be redesigned to meet these needs.

Based on the data from the usability walkthrough evaluations, the team then decided to conduct an empirical laboratory evaluation of the two authoring methods within the tool in Phase 4. The goal of the research was to understand the usability of the two authoring methods in the tool and a third method, a control condition that allowed users to enter privacy policies in a text processing window in any format they were satisfied with (see Karat et al. (2006)). We recruited internal users who had computer experience but no policy experience for the study as an initial assessment of novice use of the three methods. This research approach was extremely practical, efficient, and cost effective due to the prohibitively expensive cost of recruiting and bringing policy experts, a rare resource, to the controlled laboratory setting. We had each of the participants read three different pre-defined scenarios about a health care, finance, and government situation, and then create the privacy policy rules that were needed to address the situation presented. Each solution required 5 or 6 policy rules to be written. Each participant used all three authoring methods. One analysis of the data we will highlight here is the scoring of the privacy policy rules the participants created for quality in terms of completeness as compared to the known solution for the scenario. A key research approach is to know what analyses you will be completing to address your research questions and hypotheses before you collect your data. We created a standard scoring metric for the policy rules authored by participants so that we could compare the data across conditions. This helped us greatly in scoring the data. The end-to-end procedure for a research study can be improved through pilot testing.

After the empirical study in Phase 4, the team next collaborated with the sponsoring organization on the release of the IBM Secure Perspective product based on the SPARCLE prototype. The prototype code and documentation we created were transferred to the sponsoring product organization as a research product deliverable. We worked with the development team to resolve issues during the integration of the core code into the product. We continued with research to enhance the functionality while the development team completed additional simulation, compliance, and administrative functionality. IBM Secure Perspective Release 1 was generally available on the i5/OS in May, 2007. Release 1V2 on Windows, AIX, DB2, and i5/OS was available in October, 2007. A crucial approach that made this work successful was that our team had an ongoing collaborative relationship with the product development team. We believed that we were all in it together. So, when there was a question about how something worked, or an issue arose, we worked together with the development team. Together, we came up with new ideas as well. This collaborative relationship continued for a number of years.

As the major work on the first release of the product was completed, a new research phase began. Phase 6 involved the team's collaborations with people in academia, industry and government in two major projects. These efforts have been focused on improving and generalizing the technology to new areas. The first was called the Open Collaborative Research (OCR) Project on Security and Privacy Policy Frameworks. The second is called the International Technology Alliance (ITA).

The OCR focused on creating an integrated privacy and security policy management framework that encompassed end-to-end solutions for data in heterogeneous configurations. The teams from CMU, Purdue, and IBM had ongoing technical conversations that defined a set of projects that different subgroups spanning the three organizations completed research. This research involved computer science, policy analysis and the design and creation of new prototypes that were tested with target users.

The ITA project is a multiyear international effort supported by the US Army Research Lab and the UK Ministry of Defence. The program includes collaborations among 22 organizations in industry, academia, and government. There are four main research areas. Our team contributed to the area on security across a system of systems. The purpose of our fundamental research was to explore new ideas about how to author and manage policies within mobile ad hoc networks (MANETS) in rugged situations. The team contributed to the first two years of the project by exploring new methods of authoring and managing policies and building new concept prototypes that were reviewed and discussed with representative users.

## 4.5    HCI RESEARCH RESULTS AND IMPACT

From the email survey, our team learned that while there were some differences in the top privacy concerns of representatives from government and industry, there was a lot of common ground in concerns and requirements for privacy technology. For example, for the industry respondents, the top privacy concern involved "The economic harm that would result to this company if a privacy breach regarding customer data became public." In contrast, government respondents stated that "keeping external users from violating the privacy of others' data" was their top concern. Industry and government shared two of the top three concerns. These were "keeping internal employees from violating the privacy of other's data" and "protecting the privacy of legacy data from unauthorized review or use." For most business organizations, their brand is priceless. Thus, possible economic harm to their businesses due to the adverse publicity that privacy breaches generate was the top concern for these respondents. Government respondents did not see economic harm as a top privacy risk. Industry and government respondents were concerned about the misuse of PI by their own employees and from external users (i.e., hackers).

The second question addressed the privacy functionality desired by respondents to address their top privacy concerns. Industry and government shared the four top-ranked choices, although they were ordered differently. The top-ranked privacy functionality included "one integrated solution for legacy and Web data," "application-specific privacy policy authoring, implementation, auditing, and enforcement," "the ability to associate privacy policy information with individual data elements in a customer's file," and "privacy protection for data stored on servers from IT staff with no need to view data content."

The in-depth interviews with a sub-sample of the respondents in phase two helped to identify a more complete set of the privacy functionality requirements through examples of the flow of PI through their business processes. On the basis of these requirements, the team then designed and iterated on the SPARCLE prototype.

During the survey and interview research, many of the participants indicated that privacy policies in their organizations were created by committees made up of business process specialists, lawyers, security specialists, and information technologists. Based on the range of skills people with these roles generally possess, we hypothesized that some flexibility and different methods of defining privacy policies would be necessary for the tool to be usable across the range of roles. SPARCLE was designed to support users with a variety of skills by allowing individuals responsible for the creation of privacy policies to define the policies using natural language with a rule guide to describe privacy rules (see Figure 4.2 below) or to use a structured format to define the elements and rule relationships that will be directly used in the machine-readable policy (see Figure 4.3). We designed SPARCLE to keep the two formats synchronized at all times. When users, who prefer authoring with natural language, finish typing in their policies and click 'save and continue,' SPARCLE invokes the natural language processing technologies that transform policies into a structured form that authors can review and finalize. This transformation provides a machine-readable format such as XACML or CIM-SPL for the enforcement engine to use (OASIS Standard, 2005).

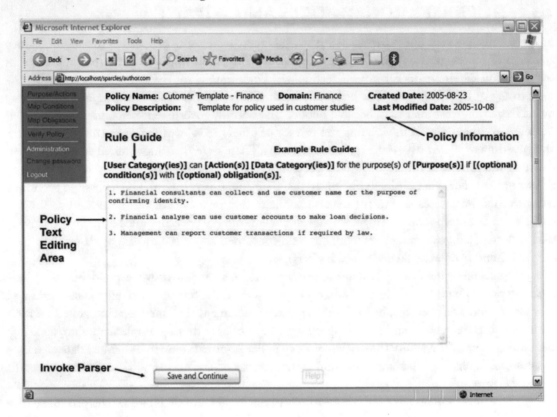

**Figure 4.2:** SPARCLE NL authoring with guide interface.

For those users who prefer to use the structured method illustrated in Figure 4.3, they simply click to select elements and compose the policy sentences. SPARCLE provides the composed policies in a textual display with the highlighted elements below for the users to review and approve before continuing. Again, a machine-readable version is available for the enforcement engine. SPARCLE also provides a policy visualization function for users to employ individually or in group review sessions to facilitate the 'big picture' view of the policy. The two-by-two chart visualization assists users in seeing the full scope of a policy or policies and identifying gaps through review of the representation (see Figure 4.4). Users can select the elements to be shown on the two axes and thus can hone in and answer questions about who has access to what. We designed the SPARCLE interface so that two or more policies could be viewed concurrently to identify issues within and between policies. In another step, users can employ the policy analysis function in SPARCLE to

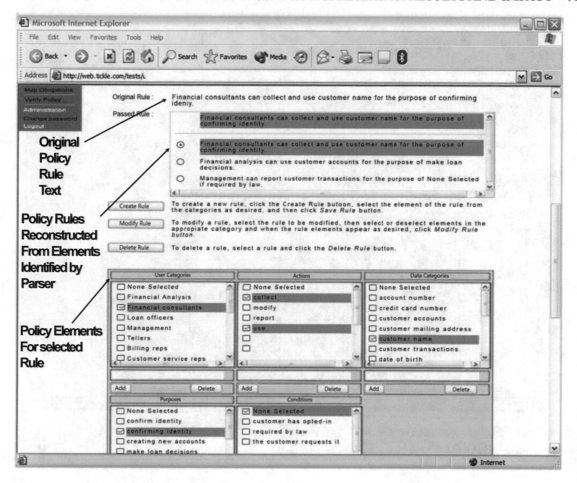

**Figure 4.3:** SPARCLE structured list policy authoring interface.

discover conflicts and redundancies within and between policies. Users are provided assistance in resolving issues, and then run the analysis routines again to ensure the policies are clear and correct. Then users employ mapping functionality in SPARCLE to tie the policy elements to the system objects. The mapping task is most likely completed by roles in the information technology (IT) area with input from the business process experts for different lines within the organization. Finally, after policies are deployed, SPARCLE provides internal compliance or auditing officers with the ability to create reports based on logs of accesses to PI.

Over three years, our team created, designed and implemented prototype functionality of the policy features described above.

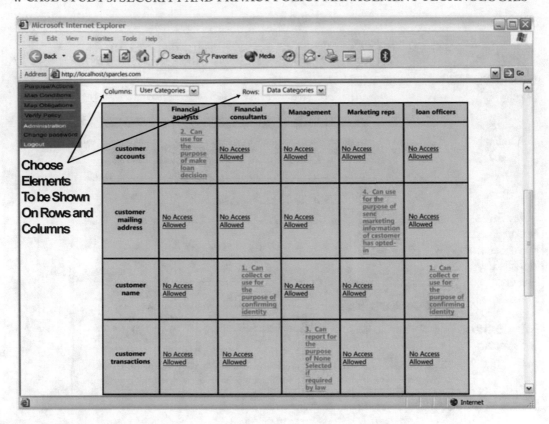

**Figure 4.4:** SPARCLE policy visualization interface.

Each year the team completed usability walkthrough evaluations onsite at target user locations with the updated prototype and functionality as it moved towards completion. The user results from the separate samples of these users across three years are shown in Figure 4.5 below.

The data show that the different samples of users were quite consistent across the three years in the positive evaluation of key functionality provided by the policy authoring prototype. The two methods of authoring – Natural Language (NL) and Structured Entry were both seen as highly valuable. Also, policy coverage visualization was rated by customer participants as a key feature.

The series of iterative prototypes and the usability walkthrough evaluations were crucial in giving the team necessary target user feedback on the functionality and interaction methods in the policy technology. We were able to validate key requirements and refine them based on situated in-context conversations about use of the technology in business operations. We learned about the set of functionality that needed to be provided to form the core of usable and effective policy technology. Many of these key features are documented in Figure 4.5.

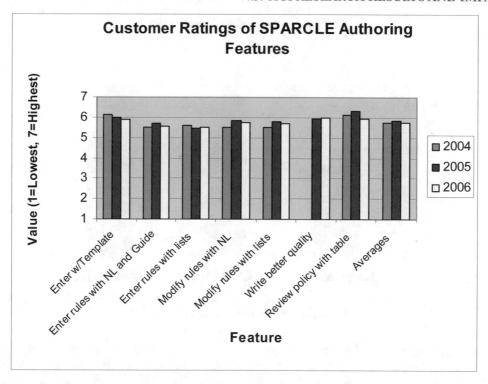

**Figure 4.5:** 2004-2006 authoring results on comparable features.

Another area of complementary HCI policy research the team conducted was the empirical laboratory testing of the policy authoring methods. The study evaluated the methods through analysis of user performance and preference data regarding the methods. In terms of the chronological sequence of events, this empirical laboratory testing was completed in parallel with the usability walkthrough evaluations of the prototype conducted in the field with target customers in Canada, Europe, and the US. Again, there was a wealth of data from the laboratory study. We highlight only a fraction of the results for illustrative purposes here. Figure 4.6 displays some of the key results from the research regarding user performance in creating policy rules.

These data demonstrate that users were able to create policy rules of significantly higher quality with the two experimental methods (NL with Guide and Structured List) as compared to the control condition method (Unguided NL). The control condition represented the current method used in everyday business situations. From the qualitative data in this study, we learned from the users that including both experimental methods in the tool would be the most promising, as users employed both methods at different points in the policy creation process. These results provided concurrent

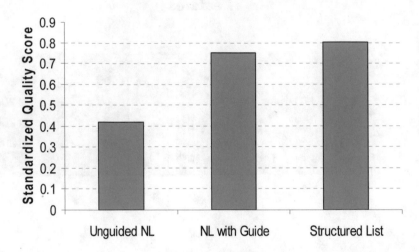

Figure 4.6: User performance with policy authoring methods.

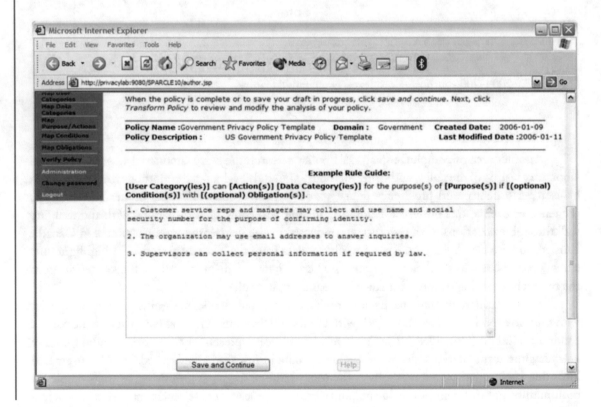

Figure 4.7: NL with guide policy authoring in the SPARCLE prototype.

validity as user preference for both experimental authoring methods in the tool surfaced in usability walkthroughs of the prototype in customer locations.

These data together helped shape the product that was developed based on the prototype. Our team collaborated with the development team in the creation of the IBM Secure Perspective product (IBM Secure Perspective, 2007). The development team added standard and innovative additional functions around required the policy prototype to create a complete and robust product. The look and feel of the product was very similar to the prototype though. Figures 4.7 and 4.8 display sample screen shots of the same functionality as designed in SPARCLE prototype and the IBM Secure Perspective product.

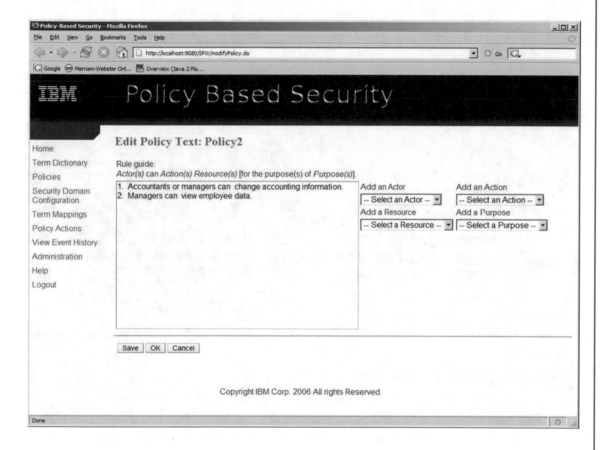

Figure 4.8: NL with guide policy authoring in IBM Secure Perspective.

As the team began collaborating with partners in academia on the OCR project, one of the ideas that we pursued was how to scale the visualization of policy for large systems with hundreds or thousands of policies. Previous research on this topic at IBM that was labeled expandable grids was brought into the OCR and explored further. Figure 4.4 above shows how a number of policies can be compared. To handle a much larger number, we experimented with the grids shown in Figure 4.9 below.

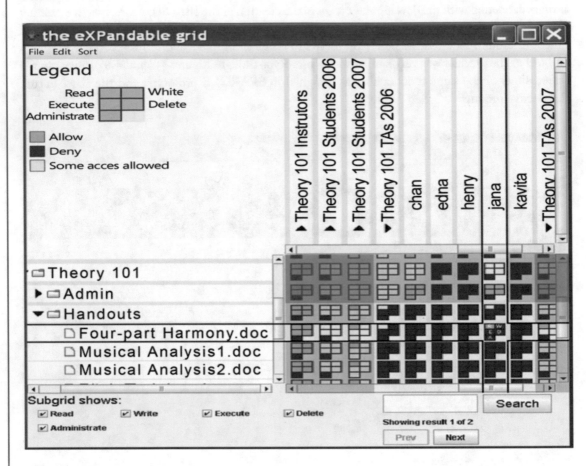

Figure 4.9: Expandable grid visualization for policies.

The idea with the expandable grids was that you could provide a user a high-level view of policies through a grid with color coding, and then you could enable drill down into areas of interest for more refined, detailed data to answer questions.

In the OCR project, we also tackled the challenge of creating a security and privacy policy architecture and explored means of enabling different types of analyses of policies (Bertino et al., 2009; Karat et al., 2009).

In the most recent ITA project, the team collaborated with other groups in industry, government and academia on policies for security across a system of systems. In this fundamental research, we considered different hypotheses and created concept prototypes to explore ideas for how coalition groups might handle security policies issues across a mobile ad hoc network (MANET) where there are people from different backgrounds, cultures, and speaking different languages working together in rugged, hostile terrain. An illustration of the high level view of the aspects of policy management in these situations is provided in Figure 4.10 below.

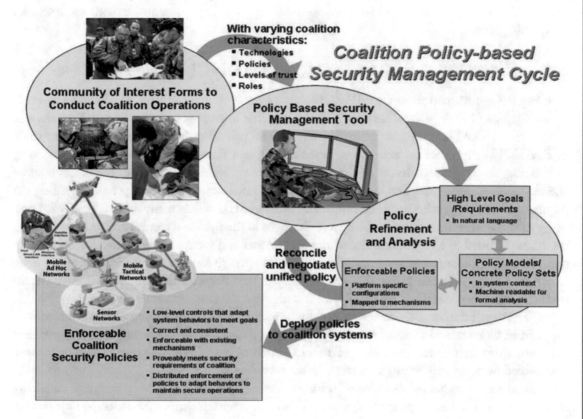

**Figure 4.10:** Aspects of policy management in the ITA project.

We explored fundamental research issues and created three different concept prototypes over the years. Research issues framing the first year's research and prototype are discussed in (Brodie et al., 2008).

In this research, we have learned that with a new view of the problem space and different requirements to consider, new possibilities for simpler and easier policy authoring are possible. Our concept prototypes are demonstrating new methods for policy management in this domain using a technique we call templates. We have also conducted research to enable the creation of new templates through a simple and usable GUI that eliminates the need for users to learn dedicated programming tools. These new policy authoring and management techniques have been successfully tested to enable the dissemination of policies to sensors and the management of the policies on these distributed sensors over time and varying conditions.

Early results are very promising, and further fundamental and more applied projects are now underway to further explore these ideas. It is possible that there may be ways to successfully generalize these new simpler policy technology capabilities into other civilian areas including energy conservation and water use to aid with the environment, and for popular applications such as social networking sites.

## 4.6    LESSONS LEARNED FROM THE HCI RESEARCH

The big lessons learned from the SPARCLE policy research and the later collaborative research in the OCR and ITA projects are that it is very valuable to employ a variety of usability methods in the research and development of usable security and privacy policy technology. The case study of SPARCLE illustrates an example of an unfolding and flowering landscape. We started with identifying the top user concerns and requirements. As we learned more about the target users of the technology, their tasks, and the context of use, we enriched the knowledge base regarding the requirements for the technology and informed details in trade-offs in many design decisions. Thus, using email surveys, interviews, usability walkthroughs in the field, and controlled laboratory testing methods provided us a means of triangulating on the user and system requirements for the security and privacy technology. Measure something that you need to know a few different ways to hone in on a valuable understanding of that area. There will be differences in your results using different methods, but over time the noise will fall away and reveal the true aspects in play.

The use of the core user scenarios was critical to our team's success. The scenarios, created with input from target users in the initial email surveys and interviews, and then validated and enriched over time through interaction with target users in laboratory and field settings, kept the team focused and helped us make many design decisions as we moved along the path.

The scenarios helped us to consider interaction methods such as natural language authoring because of the clear requirements that emerged about the characteristics of the users in the medical, financial and government settings and the processes they used to create policies in their organizations.

Another lesson involved the tradeoffs in the design decisions. We had the ability to consider design options such as natural language parsing technologies that many organizations simply could not consider due to the different types of expertise required. The designs considered can be 'blue sky' or limitless, and then you need to be able to rein in the ideas and find the best match in the design choices and what is feasible to do given time and resource constraints.

Our ongoing collaboration with the development team resulted in the smooth and efficient release of the IBM Secure Perspective product. The handoff from research to development should not be seen as 'throwing it over the wall.' Much is to be gained for all parties involved in collaboration. There is a natural ramping up and then easing off in terms of that collaboration. And there are benefits in the maintenance of research relationships with development over the years as different opportunities to provide HCI value to the organization arise.

It was very valuable to collaborate with peers in academia, industry and government to learn their perspectives and understand new requirements that surface in extending technologies to new domains. The cross-pollination in work on the OCR provided benefit and new HCI insights for both academia and industry. In our newest collaborations on the ITA, we have created new concepts based on learning of new HCI requirements for policy technology in a completely different setting with a very diverse set of users and tasks.

As our research moved from a focus on privacy policy, to security and privacy policy, to policy technology, we were challenged to see new possibilities and understand how our HCI approaches and designs could be generalized, and where the adaptation failed. To see beyond the ITA project to new valuable applications of the policy technology to helping the world take better care of precious and scarce resources is heartening. We had the hunch six years ago that this technology could be generalized to many different domains. More research is needed, but the path is there to move forward.

CHAPTER 5

# Insights and Conclusions

After presenting the three case studies, we are now interested in drawing some insights and conclusions across them. In Section 1.3 in the Introduction, we described industrial HCI research themes. Returning to these themes provides a good context for the ideas to be discussed now. There are points to be made about the industrial research setting and how it influenced the HCI research completed, as well as points about the value of different HCI methods and techniques employed in industrial research.

Let's first consider the framing of the HCI research question. Across the three case studies, we have illustrated the role of the industrial sponsors of the research in working with us to define the goals of the HCI research. In each case, what we were trying to do was influenced in some way by whom we were doing it for. Ralph Gomory, Director of IBM Research from 1970 to 1986, would often stress that in an industrial research setting, projects often have a dual mission of advancing science while also being valuable to the organization. We often found ourselves in discussion about how to serve both science and industry. This was challenging, but at the same time, it is something we think can be extremely valuable. Multiple perspectives are indeed valuable in setting HCI research goals and having access to people with different perspectives on what questions you should try and address can provide inspiration. Through interviews and discussion with sponsors, we were able to understand the business requirements in a domain of study. Through our professional colleagues, we were able to understand fundamental challenges in a domain of inquiry. The sponsors were able to point out key user and system requirements or issues that framed the business issue or opportunity.

To understand the user and system requirements more fully, we then turned to a variety of HCI methods including literature reviews to identify and avoid pitfalls as well as gain ideas about user and contextual requirements and potential solution paths. Making the most of our relatively large industrial research division (roughly 3000 people worldwide), we polled our peers and held brainstorming sessions to identify a wide range of issues and design possibilities. We also talked with many users whom we met through various channels including technical conferences, professional associations, peer to peer customer referrals, focus group participant recruiting firms, and referrals from product division representatives and other fellow researchers. By interacting with these users in a variety of settings – from focus groups to group usability walkthroughs to individual usability testing sessions – we learned a great deal about the target user characteristics, core tasks, and context of use for the domain of study. Over the years, we also developed a strong sense of the value of having a diversity of approaches which could be tailored to suit different contexts. Our involvement with users occurred throughout the different phases of research, with the initial contacts guiding us regarding the early user and system requirements, and then these were refined and enriched with further content as we moved into the iterative design, prototyping and evaluation stages.

One other key aspect of framing the HCI research questions involved the value of competitive evaluation. We were constantly driven by a desire to do more than just understand the use of technology, but to figure out how to make technology better suited to human needs and values. In this context, "understanding" and "making better" are both first class objectives. If you are going to do research in an area with existing products and services available, it's critical to understand the current state of the marketplace and the strengths and weaknesses of the available offerings. This information will provide important information in terms of setting the usability objectives and system requirements for the technology you will be conducting research and development activities on.

We think that framing the HCI research questions correctly based on the activities above helped in building quality into our research deliverables. Your probability of success is greatly enhanced if you have completed your investigative and exploratory work up front to really become educated and informed about the user and system issues, business aspects, and ideas and possibilities to begin with. Your interactions and discussions with users can be much richer and valuable, and you will have the "big picture" perspective necessary to be able to identify new aspects of the problem space as you continue along the path. For most of our projects, the dialog with the sponsors left us with far more suggestions for research projects than we were able to tackle in the time we spent on the work. When we finished one project and moved to a different research area as happened from time to time, the move was motivated by business and scientific reasons rather than a lack of good research ideas for follow-on research.

You and your team will need to have a high level plan worked out about the time, people, and resources at your disposal for the HCI research you will be conducting. Be aware that it is in the nature of industrial research environments that dramatic changes can happen with projects due to changes in business priorities. For example, one research project that we were engaged in that is not included here was cancelled after about a years work when the organizations that we were partnering with failed to reach an agreement on how to share the research deliverables. In another case, a line of research ended when IBM decided that the projected path from research to commercial development was simply too long.

Thus, you must be ready to adjust your plan and still complete your deliverables. For example, there are papers and other research artifacts from the two side-lined projects mentioned above that remained useful even after the driving reasons for the projects changed (see Karat, J. (2003); and Coble et al. (1997)). Your high-level plan will of course influence the time and energy to be allocated to the framing of the problem. Our experience suggests that allocating around 30% of your project time for this phase. In Figure 5.1 below, we present a rough generalization of how much effort we have devoted to various research project stages our HCI research. The time spent in framing the problem, while not usually the most visable research product, will pay you back many times over. This is not the place to cut corners. And as you are completing this first phase of framing the question, as you do in all the other phases, consider different ways to triangulate on the data in answer to key questions you are focusing on. Ask people in different roles; ask the question in different ways and through different methods. Then you will see the congruent validity or cross-validation begin to appear. These answers that then frame your research may change during your project based on external events, and you will need to be ready to adjust the questions you are addressing as well as how you undertake this research. So, one crucial insight is to be as informed as possible, and as you move ahead, be ready to consider tradeoffs in how to respond to changes in plan.

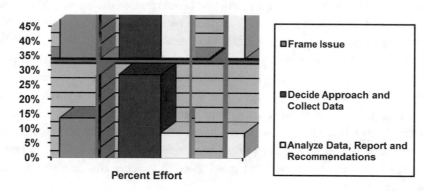

**Figure 5.1:** 1 Relative effort for HCI research project stages.

Also, establish and foster a strong relationship with your sponsor as well as future potential sponsors by understanding their requirements and how you might deliver value to them. In the SPARCLE research, our sponsor changed from year to year, and we needed to understand each person's view of the potential value of our research and other opportunities to show value. It can be annoying to have to be continually in the role of "educating your management," but viewing it as a fact of research life can help you to keep focused on long-term goals.

Beyond building and maintaining relationships with sponsors, there are similar efforts that should be considered in identifying target users for the technology. In the approach to the HCI research, one key insight is the importance of and time necessary spent in carefully identifying the users you will work with and in recruiting them to be part of your research. This can take a large amount of time. The radiologists mentioned in the development of ASR and the Chief Privacy Officers mentioned in discussing the SPARCLE work were not easily recruited. Like tending a garden, this effort takes constant care and feeding. It helps to keep in mind that it is also crucial to your success in completing high-quality research. An excellent mantra to remember on this point is that working with true representative users helps you complete high quality HCI research that is "valuable to the field and vital to the company."

In the methods used in research, we find that it is important to plan to use multiple types of methods. These can range from more lightweight and simple methods, such as email surveys, to more resource demanding and expensive methods such as group usability walkthroughs of prototypes onsite at customer locations or individual usability testing sessions in the laboratory. We've learned over our decades of research, that generally two to three iterations on a prototype are necessary to achieve an efficient, effective and pleasing interface and set of functionality in the technology. The case studies here illustrate this guideline. The approach to the HCI research and its completion may take 45% of the project schedule. Do yourself a favor and determine the statistical analyses of quantitative data and content analysis of qualitative data that you will be completing to answer your research questions before you collect any data. We are often surprised at how frequently we find work which fails to provide useful results where the failure can be traced to a lack of anticipation of what qualitative and quantitative results are required to answer research questions and enable the HCI professional to provide design advice related to them.

Design and finalize your materials with your research questions and data analysis plans in mind, and then do all the transcription and coding of your data as soon as possible after it is collected. It is amazing how quickly a researcher can "forget" exactly what happened in a particular study session. The qualitative data you collect is most understandable and clear to you and your team members right after a focus group, interview, or usability session has occurred. Transcribe and code it within 24 hours if at all possible. Use two or more raters to ensure reliability, and calculate your inter-rater reliability scores. This is another element of good research practice that is often neglected by less experienced researchers.

In the area of knowing whether you have succeeded, you will have many different ways to assess the achievement of the goal of demonstrating the value of HCI research. In Section 1.3.3 in Chapter 1 above, we listed 8 areas to gauge your success, from external publications to service to the community in mentoring students to follow and extend HCI research and knowledge. In the last 25% of your project schedule, you tie everything together in your own thinking and communicate that understanding to others. You complete the data analysis, make recommendations for your sponsors to implement, transfer research ideas and technology to your sponsors, inform the organization's strategy based on the results, provide new data to managers and co-workers on the value of HCI research, write external publications, file patents, and prepare research proposals for funding of follow-on or new research projects. To be sure, being able to secure project funding repeatedly is a clear sign that the HCI research you and your team complete in industry is valued. Repeated funding speaks, and speaks loudly. You will build an internal reputation about the value of the HCI research you and your team complete. The more value you can provide to your sponsors, by creating usable and useful technology that the sponsor can use to address a customer issue or opportunity, as well as through patents and external publications that draw interest and focus to the quality and innovation in the technology, the more your and your team's research skills will be in demand within your organization.

Throughout all of the research phases, you can also be involved in internal and external technical communities, and the HCI research you conduct in industry can influence your reputation and leadership opportunities in the field, the types of summer interns and new hires you can attract to join your team, and the types of ongoing collaboration that may occur with colleagues in academia and government. These factors might have less direct impact on the corporate bottom line, but their value can generally be successfully argued within organizations striving to influence change in technology and how people use it. We personally believe that it is vital for HCI professionals in industry to do outreach to schools and mentor students to engage and excite them about career possibilities as HCI researchers in science and technology.

# CHAPTER 6

# The Future of Industrial HCI Research

HCI research in industry has changed greatly over the last three decades. In the 1980's and into the mid 1990's, there was incredible growth and freedom in high technology industry for researchers, HCI and otherwise, in terms of their ability to determine research agendas and goals. Since the mid 1990's, the pressure of the global marketplace and the ever increasing pace of change in technology has put pressure on industrial research divisions around the world to provide quicker results in focused areas.

There are, of course, exceptions to this trend, but it is a clear trend. Research groups were formed at Microsoft as they disappeared from the phone companies. Many research divisions have been dissolved or absorbed into less research oriented R&D organizations in companies around the world. For those true research divisions that remain, there is generally now a tighter association between product and services groups and the research groups that focus on their research on those product and service domains. This association may be tied by the funding that the product and services groups provide in exchange for expected deliverables from research. Clearly, when there are expected deliverables on a schedule, there will be an impact on the type of research conducted. More research now is of an incremental nature. It extends the research on a fairly well defined path. We see this shift to incremental research in other industries as well – healthcare, pharmaceutical research, others. And having been members of NSF fund review committees, we see the proposal submissions there as generally representing incremental research now as well.

As mentioned, there are exceptions. Large, multiyear projects can free researchers to be more innovative and take more risks. Since a society's quality of life is tied to productivity, it is essential that researchers be allowed to take more risks and think 'big sky.' This is how in the past, paradigm shifts have occurred following breakthrough research. We truly hope for the health and well being of research divisions in industry, as well as for the good of society, that the pendulum swings back from its current position of incremental research to a more growth oriented portfolio of research projects with healthy amounts of risk taking on potentially valuable new technology.

What has happened in 20-plus years of HCI work in the international community? Looking back here, we see four main trends that we noticed in earlier work (Karat, J., 2003) and briefly characterize. First, the focus of HCI research and practice has moved from interface to interaction. This trend started fairly early in the history of the field, though there remains some confusion because there is still a tendency to at least talk about designing the interface rather than designing interaction (or, more currently, designing the user experience). Although there will always be work to do in designing the interface between human and tool, we have somewhat successfully moved toward an interface style that works and are moving more to broader questions of how technology fits within a broad range of human needs. These questions indicate how we interact with technology in our lives, more than they pertain to what the interface looks like.

Second, the pace of change in computing systems has shifted from slow changes in technology to rapid changes. We began our studies in the early days of personal computers at a time when issues associated with the usability of mainframe systems were still relatively important. The technology would stand still long enough for us to study it and its users in great detail. The pace of technology change brings with it some of the challenges we identified in the case studies in this book. Although behavioral science provided the HCI field with many tools and theoretical frameworks for observing behavior, these methods have generally been suited for use in fairly stable environments and not as means for providing design advice in rapidly changing ones. Newer approaches, such as integrating the use of scenarios into HCI design work, are part of the shift to approaches that fit the technological reality of the HCI design space.

Third, the population impacted directly by the technology has moved from a few users to essentially everyone. Relatively speaking, system operators and administrators are not the target audience they once were. We moved from the small group of users for whom operating a computer was their main task, to knowledge workers looking for productivity tools, to computers as providers of entertainment as well as information.

Industrial HCI researchers are increasingly as concerned about how the technology impacts the very young and the aging as we are interested in office workers. Associated with this concern is a shift to looking beyond individual activity and cognition for appropriate theoretical guidance to HCI work. Theoretical approaches such as activity theory or distributed cognition move the focus away from concentrating on the individual that has dominated HCI in the last two decades to a view of the roles of humans in a larger, interconnected world.

Finally, there has been a broadening of the industrial HCI conception of the role of technology from focusing on office work productivity to considering a broad range of use. One indication of the rise in importance of looking beyond productivity alone has been the attention given to evaluating the total user experience. This does not mean that office productivity does not deserve or receive attention; it is the focus of a great deal of human activity. However, there is an acknowledgment that activity and technology have value outside of the office and outside of narrow views of work. Value-sensitive design and considering the application of HCI methods to entertainment applications have become increasingly important.

We think that the HCI field has become increasingly diverse in the last 30 years, and that it will continue on this course. In our view, the fundamental idea in the emergence of user-centered design (UCD) was to emphasize iterative processes whose goal was the development of usable systems. As we continue to develop new terms to describe variations on the specifics of the methods we use, it seems more appropriate to stress that *partnership* in design is more critical to success than trying to identify who it is centered on. Certainly, there is general agreement that usable systems are achieved through involvement of potential users of a system in system design. But, we think that there is a need for somewhat less specificity about the exact role that users play in the design process than some people argue for. For example, in the participatory design community, approaches have been developed to enable the users to take active roles in many design activities. In the context in which these techniques were developed (Scandinavian countries with strong labor unions), users have the right to design their work environments. It is likely that techniques derived from this experience might need to be modified to fit use contexts that are different. System design is ultimately a partnership between developer and user, and the level of partnership between user and developer is a factor that will vary with organizational context. For example, the design of games is something that should involve the participation of potential users, but we do not think interaction design experts should approach game design in the same task-oriented way as they would approach an application design in banking. In our own research, we have had to work creatively to bring the voice of the user (whoever they might be) into the challenge of designing new technology. When we look at the HCI field, we are often impressed by the range of ways people are developing to bring about partnerships between people and developers.

Evaluation will always be a fundamental part of HCI research. We attempt to understand the needs of some audience and then formulate system designs to meet those needs. The focus of almost all evaluation in human-computer interaction has been on how well someone can complete some specified task using the technology being evaluated. We can measure time-on-task, observe error rates, and note task-completion rates to provide information about whether the technology is satisfactory for its intended purpose as long as there is a clear intended purpose. Measuring the effectiveness, efficiency and satisfaction of users trying to carry out tasks in particular contexts is how we define measuring usability. While there is an affective component of this measure - user satisfaction - it is generally regarded as a less powerful measure - it is "more subjective" and in the productivity-oriented end just not as critical. However, it is increasingly clear that the uses of computing technology are reaching far beyond office productivity tools. Various authors have pointed out this trend (e.g., Grudin, J. (1990); Furnas, G. (2001)) and suggested that the HCI field needs to adapt techniques to a larger scope of human activities and interests. This includes moving beyond the desktop to considering less productivity-centered aspects of human life such as providing rewarding social interactions and addressing concerns of society as a whole. As this trend continues, we see a shift in focus within the HCI field from people interacting with computers, through people interacting with information, toward people interacting with people through technology. Looking beyond the role of technology to complete a task to technology's role in making a better world takes some expansion of the focus of the field of human-computer interaction. We need to be able to ask, "Will people value this technology," and not just "Will people find this technology useful?" Measuring such value goes beyond economic notions. It should consider all aspects of a system that a user might feel makes owning and using it important. Such benefits can be identified, measured, and given a role in HCI design (Landauer, T., 1995; Putnam, R., 2000; Resnick, P., 2001).

As we move forward, the specific goals a user has in mind when approaching technology will become more varied and less easily identified. Topics such as appearance and aesthetics will play an increasingly important role in HCI design (Laurel, B., 1993; Karvonen, K., 2000). HCI professionals will need to be able to respond with something other than a blank stare when asked to assist in the design of artifacts that provide emotionally satisfying user experiences. Style (e.g., form factor, color and materials used) is becoming increasingly important to the design of standard personal computers. Devices for entertainment that "connect to the net" are becoming widespread. Newer uses of technology call for a better understanding of how people will view the technology as acceptable. It calls for approaches that are not all "efficiency of task completion" oriented. There are questions we should consider:

- How can we design a user experience that is engaging?

- When will people buy something because of its image?

- How can we measure the social value of technology?

Two interesting trends have created new opportunities for behaviorally-oriented work. One is the movement of the technology out of the workplace and into the home and everyday lives of people. While people certainly do spend some resource on labor saving devices for the home like dishwashers and such, few customers consider such economic issues when making purchases of most of the things they surround themselves with outside of the work environment. Did you really consider the effectiveness and efficiency of lighting fixtures, furniture, home entertainment equipment and such when deciding on these purchases? The second trend is to consider a wider role for technology systems in the workplace than the HCI field has traditionally assigned to workplace tools. Can technology enhance collaboration? Can it change what it means to work together on common goals? Can technology improve my quality of life?

We think these trends emphasize a new challenge to HCI research and practice. It just isn't possible to always find a measurable objective task to orient HCI engineering methods toward making easier or more efficient. It will take more than just asking if someone is "satisfied" with an experience to trying to understand more fully why they might "value" it - where value can suggest a number of considerations (e.g., ethical issues in Nardi and O'Day (1999)). What makes someone like playing a game? Why do people spend hours in chat rooms? If HCI professionals are to consider answering these questions as a part of the HCI field - and this certainly seems like a topic that HCI should consider – practitioners must become better equipped to address the affective side of value. While the field might still have a long way to go in making user centered design common practice, the basic tools for task analysis and performance measurement are already well covered, as can be seen in many chapters in this book and the general focus in the usability field. It is possible that many in the field feel that there are aspects of personal choice and value that can not be easily subjected to the usability engineering approaches of task-based systems. It is not argued that furthering the practice of use-based evaluation is the only means for advancing such systems - only that it is an area that could benefit their design and development through "normal science" (Kuhn, T., 1996).

One alternative would seem to be to declare such issues as outside of the scope of the field. This is certainly an option for anyone who feels that the challenges of designing usable functional systems sufficiently challenging. While adopting evaluation techniques to cover affective areas certainly does offer significant challenge and attention, the human-computer interaction field does seem to be the right home for these new challenges, and many within it will be interested in this direction.

Design has emerged as a central focus within HCI. The HCI field is increasingly interested in the design process: how it should proceed and who needs to take part in it? The field has discovered that there are many views on what the term "design" means and different ways to view the measurement of quality of a design. For most people within the HCI community, "good design" still implies a sense of "fitting a purpose" that can be empirically validated. As the field moves more toward considering systems that people value for purposes other than as tools, industrial HCI researchers are finding an increasing need to consider aesthetics and other factors that can contribute to the value of a system or an artifact. The contribution of "satisfaction" to the usability equation is receiving increasing attention.

We hope that these case studies have stimulated your interest in HCI research in industry. By discussing the case studies of these projects, we have given you an inside look at industrial HCI research in action, and have provided a 'big picture' view of a career in this field. We have enjoyed, been thrilled, faced challenges, handled adversity, gained wonderful insight, met and collaborated with some of the best scientists in the world, and are very grateful for all the experiences and opportunities the life of an HCI scientist in industry has enabled. We wish you all the best of luck in your adventures in industrial HCI research!

# Bibliography

Adams, A. and Sasse, A. (2001) Privacy in Multimedia Communications: Protecting Users, Not Just Data. In A. Blandford, J. Vanderdonkt and P. Gray [Eds.]: People and Computers XV - Interaction without frontiers. *Joint Proceedings of HCI2001 and ICM2001*, Lille, Sept. 2001. pp. 49–64. Springer. 58

Anton, A., He, Q., and Baumer, D. (2004) The complexity underlying JetBlue's privacy policy violations. *IEEE Security and Privacy*. August/September, 2004. DOI: 10.1109/MSP.2004.103 62

Ashley, P., Hada, S., Karjoth, G., Powers, C., and Schunter, M. (2003). *Enterprise Privacy Architecture Language (EPAL 1.2)*. W3C Member Submission dateMonth11Day10Year200310-Nov-2003. http://www.w3.org/Submission/EPAL/. 61

Anupam, V., Hull, R., and Kumar, B. (2001). Personalizing e-commerce applications with online heuristic decision making. *Proceedings of the tenth International World Wide Web Conference on World Wide Web*. New York: ACM, 296–307. 31

Arent Fox, (2003). Online Privacy Law. http://www.arentfox.com. 38

Barrett, R., Maglio, P., and Kellem, D. (1997). How to personalize the Web. *Proceedings of CHI'97* (Atlanta, GA, March, 1997). New York: ACM, 75–82. DOI: 10.1145/258549.258595 31

Berreby, D. (1999). Getting to Know You. Special Report: The Rise of eBusiness. *IBM Research Magazine*, 1, 1–4. 37

Bertino, E., Brodie, C., Calo, S., Cranor, L., Karat, C., Karat, J., Li, N., Lin, D., Lobo, J., Ni, Q., Rao, P., and Wang, X. (2009). Analysis of privacy and security policies. *IBM Journal of Research and Development*, 53, 2, 3, 1–18. 58, 76

Beyer, H., and Holtzblatt, K. (1998). *Contextual Design*. San Francisco: Morgan Kaufman. 36

Brodie, C., George, D., Karat, C., Karat, J., Lobo, J., Beigi, M., Wang, X., Calo, S., Verma, D. (2008). The Coalition Policy Management Portal for Policy Authoring, Verification, and Deployment. *Proceedings of the IEEE Policy Conference*, 1–3. DOI: 10.1109/POLICY.2008.25 58, 77

Brodie, C., Karat, C., and Karat, J. (2006). An Empirical Study of Natural Language Parsing of Privacy Policy Rules Using the SPARCLE Policy Workbench. *Proceedings of the 2nd Symposium on Usable Privacy and Security, SOUPS 2006*. ACM Digital Library, 1–12. DOI: 10.1145/1143120.1143123 57

Brodie, C., Karat, C., and Karat, J. (2004). Usable Security and Privacy: A Case Study of Developing Privacy Management Tools. *IEEE Symposium on Security and Privacy*, Berkeley, CA, May. 56, 57

Brodie, C., Karat, C., Karat, J., and Feng, J. (2005). Usable Security and Privacy: A Case Study of Developing Privacy Management Tools. In the *Proceedings of the 2005 Symposium on Usable Privacy and Security*, ACM Digital Library, July, 1–12. DOI: 10.1145/1073001.1073005 57

Burke, R. (1999). Integrating Knowledge-Based and Collaborative-Filtering. In *Proceedings of AAAI 1999 Workshop on AI and Electronic Commerce*. 14–20. 31

Calo, S., Karat, C., Karat, J., Lobo, J., Craven, R., Lupu, E., Ma, J., Russo, A., Sloman, M., and Bandara, A. (2010). Policy Technology for Security Management in Coalition Networks. In Verma, D. (Ed.) *Network Science for Coalition Operations, IGI Global*, in press. 58

Coble, J., Karat, J., and Kahn, M., (1997). Maintaining a focus on on user requirements throughout the development of clinical workstation software. CHI '97 Conference Proceedings, ACM: New York, 170–179. DOI: 10.1145/258549.258698 82

Computer Research Association, (2003). CRA Conference on "Grand Research Challenges in Information Security and Assurance". http://www.cra.org/Activities/grand.challenges/security/. November 16–19, 2003. 58

Cheng and karat (2002). 12

Cranor, L. (2002). *Web Privacy with P3P.* Cambridge: O'Reilly. 60

Duda, R. O., Hart P., and Stork, D. G. (2001). *Pattern Classification*, New York: John Wiley and Sons, Inc. 31

Danis, C., Comerford, L., Janke, E., Davies, K., DeVries,, J. and Bertrand, A. (1994). StoryWriter: A speech oriented editor. In C. Plaisant (Ed.) Human Factors in Computing Systems - CHI'94 Conference Companion. ACM: New York, 277–278. 15

Danis, C. and Karat, J. (1995). Technology-driven design of speech recognition systems. In G. Olson and S. Schuon (eds.) Symposium on Designing Interactive Systems (DIS 95). ACM: New York, 17–24. 12

Duda, R. O., Hart P., and Stork, D. G. (2001). *Pattern lassification*, New York: John Wiley and Sons, Inc.

Furnas, G. W. (2001). Designing for the MoRAS. In J. M. Carroll (Ed.) Human-Computer Interaction in the New Millennium. Reading, MA: Addison Wesley. 89

Godin, S. (1999). *Permission marketing: turning strangers into friends, and friends into customers.* New York: Simon and Schuster. 32, 39

Gould, J. D., Conti, J., and Hovanyecz, T. (1983). Composing letters with a simulated listening typewriter. Communications of the ACM, 26, 4, 295–308. DOI: 10.1145/2163.358100 16

Grudin, J. (1990). The computer reaches out: The historical continuity of interface design evolution and practice in user interface engineering. Proceedings of ACM CHI'90 Conference on Human Factors in Computing Systems. 261–268. New York: ACM. DOI: 10.1145/97243.97284 89

Hagen, P.R. (2000). Personalization versus Privacy. *Forrester Report*, November, 1–19. 39

Halverson, C. A., Horn, D. A., Karat, C. and Karat, J. (1999). The beauty of errors: Patterns of error correction in desktop speech systems. In Sasse, M. A. and Johnson, C (Eds), Human-Computer Interaction - INTERACT '99, IOS Press, 133–140. 12, 16

Heer, J., and Chi, E. H. (2002). Separating the swarm: Categorization methods for user sessions on the web. *Proceedings of CHI 2002* (Minneapolis, MN, April, 2002). New York: ACM, 243–250. DOI: 10.1145/503376.503420 31

IBM Secure Perspective, (2007.)
http://www-03.ibm.com/systems/i/advantages/security
/rethink_security_policy.html. 59, 62, 75

Karat, C., Blom, J., and Karat, J. (Eds.) (2004). *Designing Personalized User Experiences in eCommerce*. Kluwer, The Netherlands. DOI: 10.1007/1-4020-2148-8 56

Karat, C., Brodie, C., and Karat, J. (2003). Views of Privacy: Business Drivers, Strategy and Directions. IBM Research Report (RC22912). Selected for review by the *National Academy Privacy in the Information Age Working Group*, August. 57

Karat, C., Brodie, C., and Karat, J. (2005). Usability design and evaluation for privacy and security solutions. In Cranor, L. and Garfinkle, S. (Eds) *Designing Secure Systems that People Can Use*. O'Reilly and Associates, 47–74. 34, 56, 57, 58, 60

Karat, C., Halverson, C., Horn, D., and Karat, J. (1999) Patterns of entry and correction in large vocabulary continuous speech recognition systems. Proceedings of CHI 99, p. 568–575. DOI: 10.1145/302979.303160 12, 16

Karat, C., Karat, J., and Brodie, C. (2005). Why HCI Research in Privacy and Security is Critical Now. In the *International Journal of Human Computer Studies*, 63, 1–2, 1-5. DOI: 10.1016/j.ijhcs.2005.04.016 58

Karat, C., Brodie, C., and Karat, J. (2007). Usable Privacy and Security for Personal Information Management. *Communications of the ACM*, 49, 1, 56–57. DOI: 10.1145/1107458.1107491 57

Karat, C., Karat, J., and Brodie, C. (2007). Management of Personal Information Disclosure: The Interdependence of Privacy, Security, and Trust. In Jones, W. and Teevan, J. (Eds.), *Personal Information Management*, University of PlaceNameWashington Press, 249–260. 57

Karat, C., Karat, J., Brodie, C., and Feng, J. (2006). "Evaluating interfaces for privacy policy rule authoring," *Proceedings of the Conference on Human Factors in Computing Systems – CHI 2006*, ACM Press, pp. 83–92. DOI: 10.1145/1124772.1124787 56, 57, 67

Karat, C., Karat, J., Vergo, J., Pinhanez, C., Reicken, D., and Cofino, T. (2002). That's entertainment! Designing streaming, multimedia web experiences. *International Journal of Human-Computer Interaction, 14*, 3 and 4, 2002, 369–384. DOI: 10.1207/S15327590IJHC143&4_06 56

Karat, C., Pinhanez, C., Karat, J., Arora, R., and Vergo, J. (2001). Less Clicking, More Watching: Results of the Iterative Design and Evaluation of Entertaining Web Experiences. *Human-Computer Interaction - INTERACT 2001*. IOS Press, 455–463. 56

Karat, J. (1995). Scenario use in the design of a speech recognition system. In J. Carroll (Ed.), Scenario-based design. New York: Wiley. 12

Karat, J. (1997). User-Centered Software Evaluation Methodologies. In Helander, M. G., Landaur, T. K. and Prabhu, P. V. (Eds.), Handbook of Human-Computer Interaction, 2nd ed. Amsterdam: Elsevier/North Holland, 689–704.

Karat, J. (2003). Beyond task completion: Evaluation of affective components of use. In Jacko, J. and Sears, A. (Eds.), *The Human-Computer Interaction Handbook*, Erlbaum Associates, 1152–1164. 56, 82, 87

Karat, J., and Karat C. (2008). An Organizational View of Pervasive Computing: Policy Implications for Information Exchange. *Social Science Computer Review.*, 26, 1, 13–19. DOI: 10.1177/0894439307307681 56, 58

Karat, J., and Karat, C. (2003). That's Entertainment! In Monk, A., and Blythe, M., (Eds.), *Funology: From Usability to Enjoyment*. Kluwer: The Netherlands, 125–137.

Karat, J., and Karat, C. (2003). The evolution of user-centered focus in the human-computer interaction field. IBM Systems Journal, 57, 42, 4, 532–541.

Karat, J., Karat, C., Bertino, E., Li, N., Ni, Q., Brodie, C., Lobo, J., Calo, S., Cranor, L, Kumaraguru, P., and Reeder, R. (2009). Policy Framework for Security and Privacy Management. In *IBM Journal of Research and Development*, 59, 2, 1–14. 58, 76

Karat, J., Karat, C., and Brodie, C. (2008). Human-Computer Interaction Viewed from the Intersection of Privacy, Security, and Trust. In Jacko, J. and Sears, A. (Eds.), *The Human-Computer Interaction Handbook, Second Edition*, Erlbaum Associates, 640–658. 58

Karat, J., Karat, C., Brodie, C., and Feng, J. (2005). "Privacy in information technology: Designing to enable privacy policy management in organizations," *International Journal of Human-Computer Studies.* 63, 2005, 1–2, 153-174. DOI: 10.1016/j.ijhcs.2005.04.016 57, 58, 60

Karat, J., Karat, C., Brodie, C., and Feng, J. (2005). Designing Natural Language and Structured Entry Methods for Privacy Policy Authoring. In the *Proceedings for the Tenth IFIP TC13 International Conference of Human-Computer Interaction*, 671–684. DOI: 10.1007/11555261_54

Karat, J., Lai, J., Danis, C., and Wolf, C. (1999). Speech user interface evolution. In D. Gardner-Bonneau (Ed.), *Human factors and voice interactive systems*, p. 1–35. Norwell, MA: Kluwer Academic Publishers.

Karat, J., Horn, D., Halverson, C., and Karat, C., (2000) Overcoming unusability: developing efficient strategies in speech recognition systems, *CHI '00 extended abstracts on Human factors in computing systems*, April 01–06, 2000, The Hague, The Netherlands. DOI: 10.1145/633292.633372 12

Karvonen, K. (2000). The beauty of simplicity. In Conference on Universal Usability: CUU 2000, pp 85–90. New York: ACM. DOI: 10.1145/355460.355478 90

Kidd, A. (1994). The marks are on the knowledge worker, in Proceedings of CHI '94 (Boston MA, April 1994), ACM Press, 186–191. DOI: 10.1145/259963.260346 16

Kobsa, A. (2002).Personalized hypermedia and international privacy. *Communications of the ACM*, 5, 5, 64–67. DOI: 10.1145/506218.506249 38, 58

Kuhn, T. S. (1996). The structure of scientific revolutions. Chicago, IL: University of Chicago Press. 90

Lai, J. and Vergo, J. (1997). MedSpeak: Report Creation with Continuous Speech Recognition, in *Proceedings of CHI '97*, (Atlanta GA, March 1997), ACM Press, 431 - 438. DOI: 10.1145/258549.258829 14

Landauer, T. K. (1995). The trouble with computers: Usefulness, usability, and productivity. Cambridge, MA: MIT Press. 89

Laurel, B. (1993). Computers as Theatre. Reading, MA: Addison-Wesley. 90

Mayhew, D. (1999). *The Usability Engineering Lifecycle: A Practitioner's Handbook for User Interface Design*. San Diego: Academic Press. 34

Mobasher, B., Cooley, R., and Srinivastava, J. (2000). Automatic personalization based on web usage mining. *Communications of the ACM* Special Issue on Personalization. Volume 43 Issue 8, 142–151. DOI: 10.1145/345124.345169 31

Muller, M., and Kuhn, S. (1993). Participatory design (Special issue of Communications of the ACM), Communications, ACM, 36, 4. DOI: 10.1145/153571.255960 12

Nardi, B., and O'Day, V. (1999). Information ecologies: Using technology with heart. Cambridge, MA: MIT Press. 90

Ni, Q., Bertino, E., Brodie, C., Karat, C., Karat, J., Lobo, J., and Trombetta, A. (2008). Privacy-Aware Role Based Access Control. *ACM Transactions on Computational Logic*, 16, 8, 1–35. DOI: 10.1145/1266840.1266848 58

Norman, D., and Draper, S. (1986). User-Centered system Design. Hillsdale, NJ: Lawrence Erlbaum. 12

OECD Guidelines (1980). Protection of Privacy and Transborder Flows of Personal Data. 59

OASIS Standard (2005). Privacy Policy Profile of XACML v2.0. `http://docs.oasis-open.org/xacml/2.0/PRIVACY-PROFILE` `/access_control-xacml-2.0-privacy_profile-spec-os.pdf`. 61, 70

Ogozalek, V.Z., and Praag, J.V. (1986). Comparison of elderly and younger users on keyboard and voice input computer-based composition tasks, in Proceedings of CHI '86 , ACM Press, 205–211. DOI: 10.1145/22627.22372 16

Peppers, D., and Rogers, M. (1997). *Enterprise One to One: Tools for Competing in the Interactive Age*, New York: Doubleday. 32

Perkowitz, M. and Etzioni, O. (2000). Adaptive web sites. *Communications of the ACM* Special Issue on Personalization. Volume 43, Issue 8, 152–158. DOI: 10.1145/345124.345171 31

Pinhanez, C., Karat, C., Vergo, J., Karat, J., Arora, R., Riecken, D. and Cofino, T. (2001). Can Web Entertainment be Passive? *Proceedings of IWWW '01.*

Ponemon Institute and IAPP. (2004). 2003 benchmark study of corporate privacy practices. 60

Putnam, R. (2000). Bowling alone: America's declining Social Capital. New York: Simon& Schuster. 89

Reeder, R., Karat, C., Karat, J. and Brodie, C. (2007). Usability Challenges in Security and Privacy Policy-Authoring Interfaces. In *Proceedings of INTERACT 2007*, 141–155. DOI: 10.1007/978-3-540-74800-7_11 58

Resnick, P. and Varian, H.R. (1997). Recommender Systems. *Communications of the ACM*, 40, 3, 56–58. DOI: 10.1145/245108.245121 31

Resnick, P. (2001). Beyond bowling together: SocioTechnical CapiPersonNameSametimeSmart-Tagtaltal. In J. M. Carroll (Ed.) Human-Computer Interaction in the New Millennium. Reading, MA: Addison Wesley. 89

Rhyne, J. R. and Wolf, C. G. (1993). Recognition based user interfaces. In R. Hartson and D. Hix (Eds.), Advances in human-computer interaction, vol. 4. Ablex. 15

Schaffer, J. (2001). *Personal Communications*. 40

Schafer, B. J., Konstan, J., and Riedl, J. (1999). Recommender systems in e-commerce. *Proceedings of the first ACM Conference on Electronic Commerce*. New York: ACM, 158–166. DOI: 10.1145/336992.337035 31

Schonberg, E., Cofino, T., Hoch, R., Podlaseck, M., and Spraragen, S. (2000). Measuring success. *Communications of the ACM*, 43, 8, 53–57. DOI: 10.1145/345124.345142 31

Smith, J. (1993). Privacy policies and practices: Inside the organizational maze. Communications of the ACM, 36, 12, 105–122. DOI: 10.1145/163298.163349 60

Spiliopoulou, M. (2000). Web usage mining for web site evaluation. *Communications of the ACM*, 43, 8, 127–135. DOI: 10.1145/345124.345167 31

VanderMeer, D., Dutta, K., Datta, A, Ramamritham, K., and Navanthe, S. B. (2000). Enabling scalable online personalization on the web. *Proceedings of the Second ACM Conference on Electronic Commerce*. New York: ACM, 185–196. DOI: 10.1145/352871.352892 31

Volokh, E. (2000). Personalization and privacy. *Communications of the ACM*, 43, 8, 84–88. DOI: 10.1145/345124.345155 38

Vredenburg, K., Isensee, S., and Righi, C. (2001). *User-Centered Design: An Integrated Approach*. New York: Prentice Hall. 34

# Authors' Biographies

## CLARE-MARIE KARAT

**Clare-Marie Karat** (cmkarat@gmail.com) is a Research Staff Member in the Policy Lifecycle Technologies department at the IBM T. J. Watson Research Center in Hawthorne, New York. Dr. Karat's HCI research interests are in the areas of policy, privacy, security, usability methods, usability cost-benefit analysis, conversational speech technologies, and personalization. Under Dr. Karat's leadership, the Server Privacy ARchitecture and Capability Enablement (SPARCLE) Policy Workbench research project has created innovative policy authoring and management technologies and interaction methods to provide users and organizations with effective means of managing information (www.research.ibm.com/sparcle). She also has technical leadership roles in the Army Research Laboratory International Technology Alliance (ARL ITA) project on security policy management of information in mobile ad hoc networks and IBM's Open Collaborative Research on Policy Frameworks for Security and Privacy project with academic colleagues at CMU and Purdue Universities.

Dr. Karat is an editor of the book *Designing Personalized User Experiences in eCommerce*, published in 2004. She is well-known for the *Computer User's Bill of Rights* and for creating a cost-benefit methodology for analyzing the return on investment in usability. Her editorial board memberships have included ACM *interactions*, the British Computer Society's *Interacting with Computers*, and Elsevier's *International Journal of Human Computer Studies* journals; and she has served as a reviewer for the ACM *Communications of the ACM*, *IEEE Security and Privacy* and the *IBM Research and Development* journals. She has chaired international conferences and held a variety of technical committee roles in the ACM CHI, HFES, IFIP INTERACT, and SOUPS conferences. Dr. Karat has presented keynote addresses, taught seminars, published numerous papers in technical journals and conference proceedings, and contributed to many books in the fields of HCI, policy, privacy, security, and personalization. She has been awarded a number of patents for her technical work over the years. Dr. Clare-Marie Karat was awarded the ACM SIGCHI Lifetime Service Award in 2009 and is a Senior Member of ACM.

## JOHN KARAT

**John Karat** (jkarat@us.ibm.com) is a senior researcher in the field of human-computer interaction. Over his career with IBM Development (1982-1987) and Research (1987-current) he has worked on the development of research-based guidelines and principles for user interface design (including the chairing committees for the development of ANSI 200 and ISO 9241 HCI standards), researched and advised on design collaboration (resulting in an early book on the integration of HCI and Software engineering), researched and developed speech-based systems (including the design of IBM's first large vocabulary desktop speech recognition system), researched and designed early electronic medical record systems (for Kaiser Colorado Region and Barnes Hospital in St Louis which identified many interaction aspects required for improved patient care through better records). His research also includes publications in information search and unstructured knowledge management, entertainment applications, personalization, and security and privacy. At IBM Research, he has been a researcher, project leader, and manager. John was recently co-leader of the IBM Privacy Research Institute (2005-2008), established to advance the importance of privacy issues in IT globally. He has also worked to advance industry/academic collaboration as project leader for an open collaborative research (OCR) initiative in privacy and security policy management with Carnegie Mellon, Purdue, and Imperial College (2006-2008). The IBM OCR initiative seeks to reduce obstacles to collaboration through the advancement of open systems. He has been awarded seven patents (addressing speech recognition interfaces, search mechanisms, privacy policy management, and general help systems) and received a number of internal IBM awards for invention achievement and other contributions. John has been awarded the ACM SIGCHI Lifetime Service Award and was named a Distinguished Scientist by ACM.